ICE CREAM *for* BREAKFAST

How rediscovering your inner child can make you calmer, happier, and solve your bullsh*t adult problems

LAURA JANE WILLIAMS

HODDER &
STOUGHTON

First published in Great Britain in 2017 by
Hodder & Stoughton
An Hachette UK company

2

Copyright © Laura Jane Williams 2017

The right of Laura Jane Williams to be identified as the
Author of the Work has been asserted by her in accordance
with the Copyright, Designs and Patents Act 1988.

A CIP catalogue record for this title is available from the British Library

Hardback ISBN 978 1 473 65996 4
eBook ISBN 978 1 473 65995 7

Typeset in ITC Galliard by Hewer Text UK Ltd, Edinburgh
Printed and bound by Clays Ltd, St Ives plc

Hodder & Stoughton policy is to use papers that are natural, renewable
and recyclable products and made from wood grown in sustainable
forests. The logging and manufacturing processes are expected to
conform to the environmental regulations of the country of origin.

Hodder & Stoughton Ltd
Carmelite House
50 Victoria Embankment
London EC4Y 0DZ

www.hodder.co.uk

for N, S & L,
who don't have any idea what they taught me,
and that's what makes it all the lovelier

contents

It takes a long time to become young

~ Picasso

introduction
or,
why I wrote this

In the spring of 2016 I was on the verge of the career I'd always dreamed of. For ten years I'd worked towards the publication of my first book, and finally it was happening. The dead-end 'filler jobs' I'd had in order to make rent while stealing minutes and hours to put pen to paper, the parties missed and 'no's' I'd issued and relationships thoughtlessly squandered – everything I'd sacrificed to achieve the thing that so many people talk about but so few actually do – were paying off. Words had been proofed and front covers designed and there, on the spine of a hardback, was *my* name. I did it! I had national newspapers asking me to write things for them, my photograph was in fancy magazines, and important people said my name. There was a big party to celebrate, where everyone came for *me*, and I had a living room of more lily bouquets than Elton John. It was the moment of my life. The pinnacle of so much. I'd made it.

I'm sure it would've all been incredibly exciting, were it not for the fact that I was dead inside.

I'd burned out. I didn't know I was burnt out, because by its very definition it's a sort of *slow fizzle*. Nobody wakes up one day to find creativity packed up her paint box and left with the kids, *Playfulness, Giggles* and *Fun*, poof! Just like that. No. Burnout is clever. Burnout goes slowly. Burnout blurs the edges, at first, by telling you to work harder, for longer, and suggesting that maybe sleep isn't that important after all. Burnout tells you nothing could be as important as work. 'Success.' Burnout dismantles the house bit by bit so that from the outside everything looks the same, but inside, the furniture has been moved in a way that doesn't *feel* like you, somehow, and the curtains have been drawn so it's all a bit dark. The music has stopped. It's all very *serious*.

I didn't know I'd stopped feeling the warmth of April sunshine on my face, or that I'd ceased to find things funny, or that I no longer did things simply for the pleasure of doing them, until a medical professional asked me the right questions. I hadn't noticed I sighed a lot. Got cross frequently. That everything had to have a reason. A purpose. That it all had to be *for something*. I didn't know I was miserable until my doctor told me so.

I thought I was simply an adult.

The doc explained that no, it is not normal to be exhausted and teary and work sixteen-hour days. I wasn't, she intoned, making a fuss out of nothing. What I'd done, she said, is work so hard that I'd used up all the serotonin – the happy hormone – in my body, and I'd continue to feel pretty shitty if I didn't drastically reconsider how kindly I treated myself. It's ironic, really, but out of the corner of my eye, I could see the issue of a monthly glossy that I was featured in, cited for my 'bravery' and 'daringness' in living a life that went balls-to-the-wall. Sat opposite a kind GP and telling her I couldn't properly taste food any more, I was a fraud. There was nothing bold or daring about me. Not right now. I'd forgotten how to just *be happy* – how, in fact, to just *be* – and I'd hidden that behind the foolhardy notion that that's what being a grown-up is. Hard work. Relentless, miserable, hard work.

That's not what being a grown-up is.

What happened next is a bit left-field, but when I saw an advert on GumTree for a part-time nanny for a local family, I applied for it. I don't even know why I was on GumTree looking at nannying jobs. Like I say, I wasn't paying much attention to anything in those months. I met the kids, they weren't awful – they were, in fact, cleverer than me and funny and very polite to boot – and so I told their mum and dad that I'd love nothing more than to make packed lunches for three under-elevens every morning. *Sure*, I said, *a 7 a.m. start is fine! Great!* I smiled, *£12 an hour is perfect! No worries*, I nodded, *it takes three buses and an hour to deliver everyone to their individual schools? I'm looking forward to it!* I had a bonkers nine-month period after that, in which I spent twenty-five hours a week braiding hair and playing dolls and going to the park with somebody else's children, before heading off to the BBC for radio interviews or writing a column for a national magazine. Then I'd take these children who didn't belong to me to swimming class or gymnastics. I don't think their parents ever truly understood why a writer who sometimes gets recognised at the bus stop was loading their dishwasher – because it was cash-in-hand, maybe? – but as it all worked out so well for everybody involved they didn't push the issue. I don't know what I would've said if they had. It was weird to me, too. I just knew that being around kids would . . . help. And that I've always been good at it. I used to run a children's language school in Rome and do summer camps in the university holidays. Kids have always been my natural refuge.

Anyway. I'm not saying that if you're knackered or a bit sad or overworked, you, too, should go and insert yourself as a hired help into somebody else's family – and for less money than you normally spend on an average lunch, too – but I *am* saying: holy shit! The change in me was almost immediate. From that very first day after school when the six-year-old slipped her hand into mine and said, 'Laura, will you come on the swings with me?' I started to come home to myself. I was forced to clear my mind to focus on this new, massive responsibility that had nothing to do with me and my words and my typing and my self-editing and my *career*, and by the end of week one was able to marvel, for the first time in a long time: *So this is what it is like to play, huh?*

Every day I'd find something to laugh about with them. They were hilarious, and difficult, and stubborn, wilful, opinionated children who asked questions and told me when they were upset. They fought and loved and fell over and got back up and talked shit about each other but snuggled up in a pack on the sofa when it was movie time.

Kids, I learned, they live in the present. They lose themselves in what they love. They show off. They *like themselves*. Kids are curious as default, and don't have limits because they haven't learned to think they exist, yet. Kids do whatever the fuck they want, precisely because they want to.

Kids have got the answers, man.

Acting more like a kid – being child*like*, not child*ish* – finally made me content again. I get it now. The point of it all. Kids saved me. Being more childlike saved me.

Ice Cream for Breakfast is a book, then, about all of that. About the child-like solutions three kids from North London unwittingly taught me to apply to my own adult problems, most of which were bullshit and all made up in my head, so that I could rediscover what it feels like to go full force on the delights of my own existence. This is a book about how fun is a choice, but silliness isn't a privilege. It's a right. A necessity. Let us play, or die, says I. The overly sombre alternative is no life at all.

Ice Cream for Breakfast means knowing what the grown-up rules are, and bending them for shits and giggles. For the thrill of it. Questioning what we 'should' do and doing what makes us cheerier, instead. We can't have ice cream for breakfast every day, but when we do it is naughty and freeing and cheeky and child-like. Let's all have more ice cream for breakfast – or at least behave like we have.

Divided into forty (swear-y, which isn't very child-like at all . . .) life lessons from the mouths of babes, read this from start to finish or dip in and out when you need it. It's not written in any particular order because, fuck it, you think those little monsters taught me this stuff in any kind of linear fashion? Did they heck. It was chaos, and I'm still reeling from it. Chaos doesn't have to be bad, though. They showed me that. They showed me everything.

These are notes on curiosity and play. Living in the moment and worrying less. Words about how worthy you truly are. It's a book on how children can re-teach us to use our imagination, and creativity, and locate our joy. It's a book about feeling better, by being who we are.

Which is to say, big kids at heart.

1

the difference between child-like and child-ish

Okay, before we start, let me just clarify: I cannot stand the 'baby voice'. The playing up of stupidness; acting cutsey or dumb to get away with murder. It isn't clever, or fair, or nice to be around. It's childish, both in little folks and in adults. But child-*like*? Oh, that's just a dream. There's a massive difference between the two.

Kids are new to the world. They haven't learned to be jaded and on their guard and worn down by society and all she expects. To a kid mountains are tall, the ocean is huge, everything is both a question and an answer and limitless because of it. They marvel. They wonder. They aren't inhibited because they don't know that they 'should' be. They run, they're free, they say what they think and they are boundlessly, endlessly positive.

Child-like embodies the positive, lovely side to kiddie behaviour. But childish? Is gross. Childish traits are mostly undesirable (except for on reality television, where they make great viewing.): tantrums, self-centredness, not knowing when to be serious . . . childishness in a grown man or woman is immature, and the exact opposite of charming or charismatic.

So. Let's be very clear on the difference.

Child*ish*? Bullshit.

Child*like*? Mischievous and brazen and enthusiastic as hell.

Child*like* is GREAT.

We can be *like* children, without forgetting how to be functioning, responsible adults.

Okay? Okay.

SLEEP SOLVES

(ALMOST)

EVERYTHING

2

sleep, because it all starts there

In a life where there is *always-but-always* a last round to be drunk, and this Netflix series must be binged upon RIGHT NOW lest Twitter converse about it without you; in an existence where email will be answered immediately, because your phone is, after all, *right there,* sleep becomes a luxury.

Let's sit with that for a minute. Sit with the fact that *the very thing that keeps us functioning at all is the very first thing we throw out of the window when we need it most.*

Can you imagine telling a five-year-old that? Issuing a list of jobs they must complete before they've 'earned' the 'right' to sleep?

'Okay, Timmy, I can see that you're crying at how I've cut the sandwiches into squares and not triangles because you're tired and can't think straight, but I need you to man the bastard up and pull yourself together. Look sharp, old chap. You can sleep when you're dead.'

The first rule of any childcare is: if in doubt, the answer is bed. Tantrum? Go sleep it off. Sickness? Bed. Still tired when you wake up? SLEEP SOME MORE. Does that sound dull to you? Fucking good. Because rest isn't supposed to be stimulating, dickhead. It's supposed to be the exact opposite of stimulating, *which is the point*. THE POINT IS TO STOP DOING THINGS FOR A MINUTE!!!!

Well. Many minutes, actually. Eight-hours' worth of minutes. Personally, I like to err on the side of caution and get closer to nine. But oh, – when I don't? You'll know about it. My best friend ~~demands to know~~ gently asks me, on occasions of any meltdown or panicked text or inference of irrational anger, 'Babe, how much sleep did you get last night?' The answer is nearly always, through misty eyes and a lump in my throat: 'Not enough.' A quick Google search suggests about half of us feel that we don't get to spend enough time in bed. Sad face.

The best drug in the world is sleep. Sleep will make you funnier and cleverer and nicer and prettier, and the quickest way to know if you got enough last night is to make a note of your first thought on waking up. If the alarm goes off and you reflect, 'Bollocks to this shit, I'm done,' before hitting snooze and forcefully engineering dreams about getting on a plane someplace warm and never coming back – never, ever, ever; goodbye people of the world! – hit the hay an hour earlier for the rest of the week. The day you gracefully awaken five minutes before your alarm? That's the morning your first thought won't be 'Oh, fuck.' That's the day you change your world.

Nobody should start the day grumbling, 'Awwwww, heck. Again?!'

(And if you **do** get enough sleep? Fucking good for you, sugartits. I'm proud of you. Teach us your ways.)

Most kids don't exactly leap out of bed, and I'm not saying you ever will either (soz), but kids *are* pretty pumped about what the day might have in store, because they've got the energy to be. Let's do more of that. More of the 'wow, anything could happen today, huh?' mentality that comes with proper time in bed, snoozing. A rested person is an energised person, and an energised person can master their world.

While we're on the subject of night-time, do whatever it takes to give yourself comfort in bed, too, k? It helps! Fuzzy PJs? Something to snuggle? Heated blankets or a nice lavender wheatie? Oooooh, maybe some of that fancy pillow spray that forces you to breathe more deeply and so slip into slumber more calmly! Just, you know: make the goddamn effort. Get excited about sleep.

Bedtime can be just as much an occasion as anything else. And you're worth it. You're worth the necessity of rest. Let's stop perpetuating this lie that sleep is somehow a luxury. Sleep is your *right*. Claim it.

3

making the ordinary an occasion

Speaking of making bedtime just as much of an occasion as anything else, let's look at that. At the 'anything else'. The everyday.

When I nannied, we called homework time 'Hot Chocolate Homework Club' because, predictably, we had hot chocolate as a treat for working hard.

We started to call ordering for ourselves at the counter a 'Fortune Favours the Bold' day, because the first time the six-year-old used her voice to ask for what she wanted she got a free croissant from the *very* impressed barista, and every time we needed to be brave we reminded ourselves that lovely things can happen when you are, indeed brave.

What I call a 'Ghetto Lunch' – making do with whatever you have in the fridge – became a 'Fun Lunch' for them, where it was hilarious to eat frankfurters with hummus, or crisps dipped in Branston pickle with sponge pudding for dessert. I learned that my friend Briony calls it 'Cowboy Breakfast' when there's nothing left in the cupboards, and so anything goes. I like that.

I started to do it in my 'other', non-nannying life. Give stuff names. Adults (me) get so bogged down with simply getting through a day that we (I) forget to use the fancy coffee and heat the milk, dismissing it as a waste of time or effort. We (I) think there are more 'important' things to be doing.

We eat at our desks, and make notes on tomorrow's presentation while walking to after-work beers we don't taste because we need to rush home for *insert excuse here*. Christmas is a source of stress because there's so much to do, and I don't know anybody who hasn't experienced what it's like to be going on holiday just as they're coming down with a cold, because it's their body's first chance to slow down all year.

We're so busy living we forget about being alive.

To a kid, literally *nothing* is more important than arranging their sausages and mash into two eyes and a smiley mouth. If they're gonna eat, they're gonna make it art. Everything is art for them.

A child will sit in the car and tell you in exquisitely painful detail for the whole journey exactly what they are going to do at Grandma's house, planning out how, specifically, to allocate their enthusiasm, puzzled as to why you're not as thrilled about doing 'Gardening Time' as they are. And we encourage it, don't we? Talk them through all the books they can read when the nice lady gives them a haircut, or how if they behave well at the dentist they can watch TV for a whole hour when they get home: their choice. Everything is an occasion, and it's fun for us to make it that way for them. We gotta do it for ourselves, too.

When everything is an occasion, the ordinary becomes extraordinary.

Every moment counts, then.

That's fun!

The only meaning life has is that which we assign to it; the only special moments are those which we declare so. Celebrate *your* everyday. Make Monday 'have what you want from the bakery day' and 4 p.m. on Wednesday afternoons 'sexy texts to somebody cute' time – that makes it a different kind of hump day (*geddit?! Hump? Like SEX???!!! Oh, fine. Never mind*). I challenge you to decide which is your favourite. It will probably be the bakery, to be honest, because text messages don't taste like sugared heaven, but both equal a good time.

Divide the days and weeks and months into things to be looked forward to, anticipated, rewarded. First of the month? Yay, pancakes for dinner! The night before a big family event? Ooooh, time for your bathroom ritual! You don't have to give it a silly name, but fuck: it *does* add to the appreciation of it.

Make things matter to you, like kids make things matter to them – even if it's just 'Fishcakes Friday' or a 'Board Game Bonanza' evening. Find the reason to celebrate. Fudge the excuse to party. Have moments that mean something. Buy the Easter napkins or the Valentine's roses or the 'just because' cupcakes. And above all: slow down enough to appreciate them. The world won't end if you do.

In your darkest moments it will feel like it's your job to keep the world on its axis, but I can assure you with 200 per cent certainty (because that's how I used to feel, too): she'll keep turning even if you take a moment to be silly as sin.

She won't, truth be told, even notice you're missing.

4

on slowing the fuck down

Little Tabitha gives zero shits about the bus schedule, or how important it is to get the chicken on by 6 p.m. if you want to eat in time for *Coronation Street*. Tabitha wants to pet the dog tied up outside the shop, and get five minutes on the swings because they happen to be free, and show you this really cool thing: *Look! Over here! It's a dead squirrel being eaten by a pigeon!*

Guess how many people die in the execution of the teeny-tiny moments of slowing the fuck down? Zero.

(My condolences to the squirrel, though.)

In her TED TALK *My Year of Saying Yes to Everything*, Shonda Rhimes describes learning from her children that stopping to play never, actually, resulted in 'losing' much of her precious time. She used to say no, when her children asked Mommy to get involved, because she was 'busy' and 'important' and, most crucially, stressed. But in her 'year of saying yes' she had no choice but to drop to her hands and knees with the train set, or the doll, or the Mad Hatter at the tea party. And when she did that? It turned out her kids only wanted her attention for about fifteen minutes anyway. Those fifteen-minute slots forced her to slow the fuck down, be in the moment, and the knock-on effect was that for taking that quarter of an hour to play she was more focused at work when she got back to it. It made her *less* stressed.

I used to tell myself there was no time to stop for fifteen minutes and do something frivolous or *just because*, but I'd mindlessly absorb the status updates of people I never liked at school yet inexplicably follow on Facebook when I was waiting for the kids at the park. I wasted time, scrolling through timelines or in front of YouTube clips, but when I put my phone in my bag when we went to the play area, being conscious not to be the half-hearted-nanny-not-paying-100-per-cent-attention, I started to realise the importance of those fifteen minutes.

What if *you* used fifteen minutes to do something proper, for *yourself*? Mindfully?

Give yourself fifteen minutes to slow the fuck down. Steal that time at home, or at work, or on your commute.

Figure out a walk from your desk and around the block, and do it at the same time every day.

Wank! That's pleasurable!

Meditate with an app on that phone you can't put down.

Email a friend from high school.

Make a snack.

Do fifteen minutes of *nothingness*. Nothing can be something, with the right attitude.

We've forgotten what it's like to be bored. Is being a

little bored such a terrible thing? Sitting still forces us to confront some difficult feelings, because we can hear ourselves think. That doesn't mean we shouldn't do it. In fact, urm, I dare suggest that's all the more reason to listen to ourselves. The dark can be less scary once we've shined a light on it.

The happiest I ever made one of the girls I looked after is when I let her be fifteen minutes late for school because she happened to have her scooter with her, and we realised the ramps at Old Street Underground were *amazing* for gaining speed. So sod it: we ran up and down for a bit, wind in our hair and colour coming to our cheeks. I like to think the fact that she got 10/10 on her spelling test that day is related to this. I like to think saying 'screw it' to the schedule is why I had the courage to ask out a friend-of-a-friend. Life was just better that morning. Everything mattered, and none of it did at all.

Fifteen minutes. That's it. Take it – because nobody is waiting around to give it to you.

things worth slowing the fuck down for

listening to the rain in bed ~ making proper chips from scratch ~ meditation ~ kissing ~ an ice cream sundae ~ the long way home ~ puppies ~ sunsets ~ photographing the thing you'll want to remember ~ reading a poem twice, because it never makes sense the first time ~ English breakfast tea ~ hot chocolate ~ coffee with a spot of brandy ~ okay, any hot drink on a cold day ~ listening to the whole album ~ telling her she is so very smart ~ books ~ calling your mother ~ smiling, and understanding why ~ the view ~ his text message ~ a thank you ~ the one who needs you ~ the one you need ~ orgasms ~ realising the season has changed by the colours of the leaves ~ the first bite ~ crafting a sentence ~ watching a squirrel ~ thinking through the thing that scares you until it doesn't any more ~ snail mail ~

A LIST OF THINGS I'D LIKE
TO SLOW THE FUCK DOWN FOR:

1. _____

2. _____

3. _____

4. _____

5. _____

MAKE CHOICES

(choices lead to action)

5

a note about decisions

Kids make decisions on a gut-level, primal, selfish instinct, normally based only on what they want to be true in that very moment – a bit like a drunk.

Kids don't write lists of pros and cons, weigh up all the empirical evidence, or call their best friend.

When making a decision a kid allows themselves to want what they want (you're allowed to want what you want! Did you know that bit? A REVELATION!) and then they say it. Boom. Done.

'You've burned my bagel, and I don't like it burnt. It tastes black,' the nine-year-old would have no issue with telling me. 'I'd like another one, if that's okay. Please.'

'When you sing along to Spotify on the bus it's embarrassing,' the six-year-old stated plainly. 'But it's funny when you mouth the words. Can you just do that?'

'Laura, when my friend comes over, can you just let us go up to my room without bothering us? It's not cool,' the eldest once said.

The amazing knock-on effect with this – with saying what you want because you want it – is that everyone around you knows where they stand. I knew to heat the bagel on a setting lower on the toaster, and to stop singing quite so loudly (I didn't pack it in totally, because this mockingbird will not be silenced), and how to best be a 'cool nanny' in front of their friends instead of the 'embarrassing weird nanny'. The kids gave the gift of straight talking and decision making to me daily. I always knew how to serve them best, because they let me, and that felt good for me.

I mean, there's a difference between rude and honest, obvs. But I seldom felt offended by the girls' directness – I was just grateful that they let me know what they needed.

What would it be like if I said what I needed? I began to wonder. *If I let myself want what I want, too?*

Often, the scariest thing about saying what you want is confessing it to yourself. That's what I found. I was terrified to let myself acknowledge that I had needs.

Some things that even the adult-iest of adults can struggle to admit wanting – okay, fine, some things that I struggle to disclose I want – include:

- physical reassurance
- verbal reassurance
- space
- a fucking minute to get my head together
- a night off from drinking
- feedback at work
- to stop being the one who always accommodates others
- help (in any sense of the word)

- more time
- more sleep
- more money
- in fact, more full stop, because who the fuck am I to request extra of *anything*?

It's also scary to say I want:

- company – *just because*
- a favour
- affection
- time alone
- not to want to have to shoulder somebody else's burdens
- support
- that £20 back, please
- praise
- forgiveness
- an explanation
- the right to talk about myself
- the bins taking out.

I started to realise: when somebody asks what I want at the coffee shop, I *can* just say a *frappachoccowhatsathing with cream* instead of worrying what they'll think and mumbling something about a decaf Americano.

When my agent or editor or accountant or dad needs that one thing doing right now, I *can* reply that I'm busy, actually.

When a lover tries a 'sexy new thing' in bed, I don't have to pretend to enjoy it or agonise on how to break constructive feedback to them gently. I *can* simply say: 'Babe. Put the butter away, please. That wasn't fun for me.'

I guess my gut tells me what I want before my ego steps in to rationalise why I should or shouldn't want it, and nannying helped me remember that. Forgetting is how I ended up trying to be all things to all people in the first place, then failing and feeling like a crap bag of wonky dick parts. And, okay, you know, our ego can be useful sometimes – if we all jumped the fittie on the 73 bus at will, or farted when we felt like it because 'YOLO!', the world would be a sexually assault-y, smelly place. I'm not talking about listening to the rage-filled voice that says 'just get out and slap the bitch' when the asshat in a BMW undercuts you on the motorway.

What I *am* dealing with is that initial reaction to a question. The initial reaction that is inherently a heart-beat-quickening

'HELL YEAH!'

or a tummy-sinking

'OH FUCK NO!'

I started to give weight to that initial reaction. Let myself have it (oh! To let myself have it!) and then say what it was out loud. I tried not to worry what people thought of me as I practised this: with the confidence of those girls behind me, I just gave it a go.

I said 'Hell, yeah!' to going swimming at 6 p.m. every day, because it felt good to use my body in the slow, drugged way that being underwater forces from you.

I said, 'Oh fuck no!' to offers of coffee from blog readers or Twitter followers, because I could barely raise a smile for those closest to me – I certainly wasn't going to put on a show for a stranger, no matter how well-intentioned either of us might be.

I said, 'Hell yeah!' to having my best friend and her girlfriend over for dinner in the garden, and comfy shoes, and deleting emails without responding because there are only so many hours in a day.

I said, 'Hell yeah!' to therapy once a week.

I said, 'Oh fuck no!' to the voice in my head telling me I was selfish for taking time out, and to the stigma around mental health and getting medication.

If I was afraid folks would wonder who this new sassy-pants Laura was, I needn't've. People appreciate people who trust themselves enough to say what they want, I found – it takes the guesswork out of it for everybody else. People said it made them want to be more honest about their needs, too. Even my mama said that to me!

Basically, we're all looking for permission to want what we want.

Lead by example, then. The world needs you to.

WHAT ARE SOME THINGS THAT MAKE YOU THINK 'HELL YEAH!'? WHAT DO YOU WANT TO DO MORE OF, JUST FOR SHITS AND GIGGLES?

1. _____
2. _____
3. _____
4. _____
5. _____
6. _____
7. _____
8. _____
9. _____
10. _____

WHAT IS A THING THAT MAKES YOU THINK 'OH HECK NO!' AND SO YOU WILL START TO DO LESS OF?

YOU. ARE. ALLOWED. TO. WANT. WHAT. IT. IS. YOU. WANT.
YOU. ARE. ALLOWED. TO. WANT. WHAT. IT. IS. YOU. WANT.
YOU. ARE. ALLOWED. TO. WANT. WHAT. IT. IS. YOU. WANT.
YOU. ARE. ALLOWED. TO. WANT. WHAT. IT. IS. YOU. WANT.
YOU. ARE. ALLOWED. TO. WANT. WHAT. IT. IS. YOU. WANT.
YOU. ARE. ALLOWED. TO. WANT. WHAT. IT. IS. YOU. WANT.
YOU. ARE. ALLOWED. TO. WANT. WHAT. IT. IS. YOU. WANT.
YOU. ARE. ALLOWED. TO. WANT. WHAT. IT. IS. YOU. WANT.
YOU. ARE. ALLOWED. TO. WANT. WHAT. IT. IS. YOU. WANT.
YOU. ARE. ALLOWED. TO. WANT. WHAT. IT. IS. YOU. WANT.
YOU. ARE. ALLOWED. TO. WANT. WHAT. IT. IS. YOU. WANT.
YOU. ARE. ALLOWED. TO. WANT. WHAT. IT. IS. YOU. WANT.
YOU. ARE. ALLOWED. TO. WANT. WHAT. IT. IS. YOU. WANT.
YOU. ARE. ALLOWED. TO. WANT. WHAT. IT. IS. YOU. WANT.
YOU. ARE. ALLOWED. TO. WANT. WHAT. IT. IS. YOU. WANT.
YOU. ARE. ALLOWED. TO. WANT. WHAT. IT. IS. YOU. WANT.
YOU. ARE. ALLOWED. TO. WANT. WHAT. IT. IS. YOU. WANT.
YOU. ARE. ALLOWED. TO. WANT. WHAT. IT. IS. YOU. WANT.
YOU. ARE. ALLOWED. TO. WANT. WHAT. IT. IS. YOU. WANT.
YOU. ARE. ALLOWED. TO. WANT. WHAT. IT. IS. YOU. WANT.
YOU. ARE. ALLOWED. TO. WANT. WHAT. IT. IS. YOU. WANT.
YOU. ARE. ALLOWED. TO. WANT. WHAT. IT. IS. YOU. WANT.
YOU. ARE. ALLOWED. TO. WANT. WHAT. IT. IS. YOU. WANT.
YOU. ARE. ALLOWED. TO. WANT. WHAT. IT. IS. YOU. WANT.
YOU. ARE. ALLOWED. TO. WANT. WHAT. IT. IS. YOU. WANT.
YOU. ARE. ALLOWED. TO. WANT. WHAT. IT. IS. YOU. WANT.
YOU. ARE. ALLOWED. TO. WANT. WHAT. IT. IS. YOU. WANT

6

being angry for all of ten seconds

The emotion we (I) suppress most fervently is anger, because on some bullshit level we (I) don't think we're (I'm) entitled to get upset. We think 'mature' 'adults' 'just deal with things' instead of 'making a fuss'. It's not 'mature' to 'vent' and not 'attractive' to come across as 'needy'.

I call codswallop on that.

Anger can let us know what's important to us. It's an extreme reaction! Extreme reactions reflect extreme feelings! Feelings are okay!

The most startling insight I had when around the kids was how short-lived a child's anger is – and that's because they don't hold it in. They don't let anything fester. The eldest could say in one breath that she was irritated with her sister for stealing the remote, and as soon as she got it back she'd pull her in for a snuggle in front of *K.C. Undercover.* They'd bicker over who had six Midget Gems and who had four, balancing it out so that it was equal over an incredibly heated discussion that culminated in everyone being perfectly happy, even if for a hot second I'd worried otherwise. They weren't afraid to get cross or pissy, the girls, because they knew it didn't make them any less lovable, and that ultimately, it would be possible both to get what they needed and to make sure the other person did, too.

Let's not all scream loudly for ten seconds at a time when we feel cross (and, oh, *holy hell* foot stomping is my limit: foot stompers don't get my attention – foot stompers get sent to their room) but maybe let's agree that getting pissed off out loud and then carrying on with our day might actually be . . . well, healthy.

It's not about 'passing the monkey', as we call it in my family – handing off your anger by yelling at somebody else, until they get angry and you can make like Elsa and let it go.

It's about feeling it, acknowledging it and releasing it to the gods. Lightening your load.

It's really nice not to carry around anger. I reckon yelling a lot is basically the gateway to a heart attack, but learning to say the words, 'That upset me' or, 'That hurt my feelings' is fucking MASSIVE. It is also very helpful in managing further anger. Nobody pushes a person who can say, 'Ouch'. It's like kicking a puppy. So by speaking up at first riling, we're saving everyone a meltdown later. What if Britney had said 'that's enough' before she'd shaved her head? I'll bet that journalist's car would never have been totalled by her umbrella, for one. Do you hear what I'm saying? Forgiveness might be better than permission, but when it comes to anger, prevention is better than cure.

I suppose what helped me is understanding that dealing with anger in a childlike way isn't about judging yourself for feeling any one way in the first place. You feel how you feel, okay? Ain't no thang. Everyone has feelings.

I'm allowed to feel overwhelmed by expectations at work. I'm allowed to be upset by my brother-in-law's insensitive comment. I'm allowed to feel anxious about money.

What was pretty life affirming for me was starting to concede to these feelings. I had to admit to myself what hurt, or irritated, or annoyed. When I started to take a little more ownership over my anger or frustration, I found out that nobody is going to get angry that *I'm* angry or frustrated. Mostly, people just wanna help. People *want* to give us back the remote and make sure we have the same number of jellied sweets as they do; it's just that they wanna be happy, too. People don't actively try to hurt or provoke us, usually, no matter what our darkest thoughts might try to have us believe.

Everyone likes it when everyone gets along.

Any kind of extreme emotion is a display of vulnerability, and again: it takes trust to be vulnerable. But, the thing is, being vulnerable enough to vocalise discontent actually makes us stronger. That's what I found, anyway. Being vulnerable enough to say I am bothered by something – the way you just gave me that feedback, the fact that you still haven't booked the train for this weekend away, how you always talk over me when we're with our friends – forces me to put words to my boundaries. Jesus, it helps me to figure out where those boundaries might be in the first place.

Oh yah. That was a doozy of a realisation: boundaries. I hadn't gotten the memo that it was okay to have them. I thought loving, nice, amiable people didn't have boundaries. I thought that they just loved and loved and loved, into infinity. And most of the time? That's what was making me angry. That I felt the 'pressure' to always be happy and okay, even when confronted with a total bell-end.

When I began to own my anger, I understood I was really owning my boundaries. That my heart doesn't have to be so wide open that any fucker in dirty boots can trample right through it. When the nine-year-old took herself to her room to read because the youngest one was getting in the way of playing dolls, she was saying: 'this isn't okay by me'. The youngest one was taking the piss by using the 'good' doll and saving all the 'best' dressing-up clothes for herself. So her sister left her to it. The line had been crossed, and it was the nine-year-old's choice to decide where that line might be.

I can, I came to understand, have a wide-open heart and surround it with a big fucking fence, as Danielle LaPorte says. Those kids were A+ at that, and it took the full nine months of watching it for me truly to grasp how bad most of us grown-ups are with it. How much more I could do to protect my heart. But. Now that I've figured that out? How to be open, *and* protective? I feel like superwoman.

7

endless love and constant boundaries

Drew Barrymore said this in a Refinery 29 article about Oprah. 'You have to have endless love, and constant boundaries.' If you ask me, Drew Barrymore is the posterchild for what it is to embrace a child-like nature in an adult world.

I really get the feeling that to be in Drew Barrymore's company is to be in company where literally anything goes. What a vibe to have! How marvellous to be able to make anyone and everyone feel comfortable around you, because you've done the work to be comfortable with yourself. She runs her own production company, vineyard, make-up brand *and* calls most of Hollywood a friend, yet she seems light-hearted and fun. She's a business maven, and a laugh. She reckons she's that way because of boundaries.

Once you know where your boundaries are, it's easier to build a railing around them, to mark them out, so that they are trespassed against less and less frequently.

Ultimately, that will make you happier.

(It made me happier.)

It's a horrible feeling to suspect you're being taken advantage of. To feel like you're being shat on, for one reason or another. To know in your belly that you don't like how somebody is treating you, yet sort of understanding that you've not told them any differently.

You can wish your friend-of-a-friend well, without dropping your Saturday night plans to help them move house because you saw on Instagram they were struggling. If you've had theatre tickets six months in advance, you're not a bad person for simply sending them a text to say you're thinking of them, leaving it at that.

You can tell your mother that, yes, while it's awful she's arguing with her sister that way, you're actually in the middle of making dinner, so you'll have to call her back in the morning. You're not a bad son for refusing to get dragged into the drama when it's date night for you and your honey.

You can love your husband and not want him to order for you in a restaurant. You can choose your own burger, for Christ's sake.

You can give your last Rolo to the one you love, and still think it's bang out of line when they use the last of your £25 shampoo.

You can think your child is the most perfect thing ever to have been born, but still acknowledge that they're taking the piss when they don't hang up their school uniform or expect *you* to put their dirty dishes in the sink.

The notion of boundaries existing where love also does occurred to me when the six-year-old I looked after pitched a shit-fit the first time I tried to lift her. I needed her to move out of my way, on the stairs, and I guess I thought that because I am bigger I could exercise my brute strength on her. I picked her up under the arms, and shuffled her to the left. She made it *very* clear she was not for physical manhandling that way – she screamed and said, 'No! Don't do that! I don't like that!'

Can you imagine having the self-possession to say those words?

No.

Don't do that.

I don't like that.

That's *powerful*.

She was absolutely right, of course – I don't know why I thought I could do that to her. I'd asked her to move and she didn't, so I'd resorted to mild physical force. That is sooo not okay. But you know what? I never tried to lift her to make her do something again. Clear boundary. Done.

She won't remember telling me about this boundary, though. She didn't use it to fuel a grump for the rest of the day, or act pissed off. She did it – set the boundary

– and moved on. That's pretty fucking cool. She got to let her anger go, make her point, and it helped me to be a better nanny to her. Everyone won.

As much as kids want love and affection, and to give it, too, they set their limits in a way that astounds me. That is to say, they do it in a very straightforward, vocal way. 'That's not how I like it done!' they say. 'You're not my friend if you do that!' they cry. 'I already told you!' they sigh. Kids are affectionate as all hell, but hot damn they let you know where their line is. It isn't personal – it's just how it is.

Can you imagine being that way? Knowing that *it isn't personal; that's just how it is.*

When she tells you that no, you can't use her £150 Tom Ford perfume, *that's not personal; that's just how it is.*

When he says it's not acceptable to be thirty-five minutes late, *that's not personal; that's just how it is.*

When you explain to your housemate that the back door was left unlocked *again* and it's going to fuck up the insurance when you get robbed, *that's not personal; that's just how it is.*

You're not allowed to be a c**t under the guise of this, obvs, but WOAH! Giving out feedback in a way that isn't personal, and receiving it that way too? Maybe that would make us all a little less precious, and a lot fucking cheerier.

It's not personal. That's just how it is.

(sometimes, though, you do just have to say . . .)

Bollocks to them.

8

forgiveness, or something like it

A child actively wants a relationship with you; for you both to be happy. A child isn't waiting for you to screw up so that they can hold it against you; a child isn't remembering how you fucked up two weeks/months/years ago. To forgive is to move on, and we could all do with moving on from some of our past hurt. There's a lot to be said for the forgetting part of forgive and forget.

I mean, I know it's not *easy*, or always deserved. But it *can* feel like a relief.

Forgiving others – and forgetting about it – isn't about excusing *them* so much as allowing *ourselves* peace. When we forgive, it's easier to be happy or productive.

Bearing a grudge can strip us of our dignity, in many ways – letting resentment fester is a sort of mental trap. Letting resentment fester is a sure-fire way to let it grow, too. Holding it in gives it oxygen, so it keeps burning. Letting it go can extinguish the flame.

When we feel disempowered after we've been wronged, sometimes the only way to claim our power back is to set the terms of forgiveness – for ourselves. Not for them. We hold our heads higher when it's us who have decided to move on. And we're allowed to do that. Move on.

The middle child I nannied was particularly sensitive, but also very self-sufficient with her emotions. Her equivalent to active forgiveness was a shrug of the shoulders and a new game to play, alone, so she could exhale in her own time. She'd always re-join us once she'd an hour or two to move on. It gets a bit more serious as an adult, I know, with wrongdoing exceeding issues far graver than stealing pencils and refusing to play 'tag', and I've given 'why' a lot of thought.

I know this sounds wanky, but I tried writing myself a letter whenever I got upset or felt betrayed. I guess, because writing is my first language, this was the easiest way for me to find a safe space to express myself. I've taken to writing myself a letter giving myself permission to be free of what I'm holding on to. I let myself own the reality that I've been hurt – I actually write down, 'I have been hurt'. I admit something bothered me, and then release it. I write down:

I fully and freely forgive _____ **(person's name) for**

_____

(enter transgression here).

If you're gonna do this too, write it down as many times as you need to.

Maybe you're cross at your wife for eating the last of the good jam before you got back from the gym.

Maybe you're pissed off at your best friend because she doesn't call as much any more.

Maybe your mother ruined your childhood, or your father should've paid for pony lessons.

There could be a million tiny things or a million massive things bogging down your brain, but if you write them down you get to discharge them – a bit like how Dumbledore's Pensieve works in *Harry Potter*. It leaves room for all the other stuff you need room for (like maybe the courage to sound it out with a third party, if that will help you to release it further. That's okay, too!).

I forgive you.

It's so, so powerful to learn to say that. It makes me feel lighter. Weirdly, it makes me feel more in control by relinquishing control.

Forgiveness does NOT make you a doormat. I always thought people who forgave too quickly were just asking to be hurt again. The more I practise it, the more I find forgiveness is a way to keep my open heart, with that fence around it.

Forgiveness lets me breathe.

Forgiveness relieves my focus on what I'm pissed off as hell about and lets it move on to better, more useful things.

Once I've forgiven, I'm in a much better frame of mind to say, 'So, what game shall we play next?'

Sometimes, we don't get the apology we deserve. That's just the way it is.

Exhale anyway.

9

some things that you deserve

A hug. A smile. A friend who loves you. Love, period. A safe place to live. Running water, heat, clean sheets. An education. A chance. Hope. The Oreo milkshake. Sunday morning lie-ins. To know what you want. To go after what you want. To take the trip. To look in the mirror and like what you see. A new jumpsuit. To skip. To dance. To play. To leap in the name of *why not?* To just exist.

Meaning. Aliveness for aliveness' sake. Appreciation. To fuck up. To redeem yourself. The privilege of change. Travel. No judgement. To decide what success is for yourself. To shave your head, pierce your nose, to wear the tutu with the stripy tights and biker boots. The prom dress, the yuppy shirt, the rimless glasses. What-the-hell-ever. A night in. To ask him out. To ask her out. To say yes. To let them pay. To share what you have. To make something. Music. A voice. Discussion. Debate. Argument. Opinion – and the right to change it as you learn something new. Sun on your skin. Your feet in the ocean. Books. The 'cute meet'. A really great haircut.

To have everything you think you know changed in just one single moment. To treat the one you love to something they've wanted for a while. Kindness. Even more kindness. The best. Slivers of happiness. Wholeness. To feel the fear and do it anyway. To say no. To be yourself. Confidence.

The strength to walk away. Sex. Good sex. Orgasmic sex. Intimacy. Children. Family. To feel special. The perfect job. No shame. To do it your way. To ignore the haters – because there will always be haters. Romance.

Vulnerability. Consent. To own your humanness. To quit when it just doesn't fit any more. Right now. To be balls-deep in what you're passionate about.

You deserve, actually, everything you've ever dared wish for.

LET'S LIKE OURSELVES

10

liking who you are

The coolest thing I have ever known a child to say is, 'I love my daddy, and my mummy, and myself.' My friend Meriah's kid said that. Bloody well done, Meriah. That's a kid I wanna know as an adult.

I never for a second suspected the eleven-year-old of lying awake at 4 a.m. wondering if Trevor took her joke the wrong way at lunch. The youngest never fretted that she'd suitably demonstrated her ability to speak up in class, and never kicked herself for eating *two* chocolate pots at lunch. In the best way possible, those girls didn't think about other people much, because they didn't think of themselves that much. They were self-aware without being self-doubting, conscious of others without making others the centre of their own worlds. They were thoughtful, but didn't overthink.

What's that famous quote – so famous I don't even know who said it – about how it takes ages to unlearn everything you've been taught to be sorry for as a grown-up? I don't know, maybe I'm getting more than one quote confused, the more that I think about it, but that doesn't undo my point: keeping a list of reasons in the back of our minds about why, exactly, we're utterly rubbish in life and love and the universe, maintaining a chronicle of why everybody hates us, and the things we do wrong, it all zaps energy better used for, like, having fun. And what is all this for if not to have a rollicking good time?

The purpose of life is to enjoy it.

Don't get it twisted: liking yourself can be a lifetime's work. Because we learn, as grown-ups, how *not* to like ourselves, undoing that doesn't just happen once. *Ta-da! Fixed!* Oh no.

Being taught by society and through culture and gender norms and sexual restrictions and manners and 'being nice' and all that other stuff we know exists and exhausts us to fight – well, it's fucked up.

It's so fucked up, and nuanced – we have habits, so very rooted over time – that it's not possible that you'll read this and then decide to adore yourself and that's it, forever and ever amen: total self-love. That's certainly not how it's been for me, anyway.

Some days we know we're doing okay, and others feel like the world is ending, and the only thing we have to remember is that on **all** of those days we are worthy.

That's what liking ourselves is cemented in, innit? Worth.

When I taught English as a Foreign Language in Italy, I remember meeting a thirteen-year-old called Giulio who was funny and clever and obsessed with The Beatles and Woody Allen films (yes we talked about how problematic

Woody Allen is). I'd sit next to him at lunch and listen to him be excited about what he loved and saying things like, 'And of course, I would like to study in England because my English is very good.' He'd say, 'I can be a filmmaker who everyone will know the name of,' and 'My sense of humour is the best thing about my personality.' Kids have got self-worth by the bucket-load, because they haven't started on any kind of fruitless path towards perfectionism. The only path a kid is on is the one towards becoming themselves – and that's just fine.

Be you. You is awesome.

Giulio made me want to suspend judgement on myself. Be my own best friend by refusing to categorise the things I do and the thoughts I have and the way my days pass by as 'bad' or 'good'.

If you want to do the same, as your own best friend tell yourself that you are indeed worthy, and that you matter, and that you're not going anywhere. You're always going to be there for yourself.

Talk to yourself like you would do the child in your life.

'Good job!'

'Great effort!'

'Take it slow, babe!'

'Have you eaten yet?'

'You're so good at that! You must've put in a lot of effort!'

'I love you.'

Reassure yourself you're not gonna quit on who you are.

Promise yourself the love you have for you is unconditional.

The only thing that matters is that your intentions are pure and your heart is true. If your intentions are pure and your heart is true, you get to call yourself authentic, and when you're your most authentic self, you're free, darlin'.

If you need a less wanky way to think of that, try this: know you're doing your best. And your best? Is enough.

Everything you already are is perfect.

'Always be a first-rate version of yourself and not a second-rate version of someone else.'

~ Judy Garland

NINETEEN THINGS I LIKE ABOUT MYSELF

e.g. I like my hair. I like my laugh. I like how
I can read a room. I like that I remember
birthdays. I like that I am organised. I like
that I like nineteen things about myself . . .

1. _____
2. _____
3. _____
4. _____
5. _____
6. _____
7. _____
8. _____
9. _____
10. _____
11. _____
12. _____
13. _____
14. _____
15. _____
16. _____
17. _____
18. _____
19. _____

NINETEEN THINGS I AM GOOD AT

e.g. I am good at boiling eggs for egg and soldiers. I am good at tying my shoelaces right the first time. I am good at being on time. I am good at taking really long showers. I am good at using my fancy handwriting to make nice lists . . .

1. _____
2. _____
3. _____
4. _____
5. _____
6. _____
7. _____
8. _____
9. _____
10. _____
11. _____
12. _____
13. _____
14. _____
15. _____
16. _____
17. _____
18. _____
19. _____

FIVE THINGS IT DOES NOT MATTER THAT I AM SHIT AT

e.g. I am shit at maths, but own a calculator. I am shit at getting my hair coloured with any regularity, so act like my roots are supposed to be on show. I am shit at behaving with any semblance of chill in romantic relationships, but know it. I am shit at keeping chocolate in the house without eating all of it, so don't keep chocolate in the house. I am shit at Scrabble, so don't play it.

1. _____
2. _____
3. _____
4. _____
5. _____

11

being proudly obsessed, you weirdo

'Look at my miniature dolphin collection!' a child will implore you, carefree and uninhibited. And do you know what? We do. Suddenly, when a tiny person tells you all about species and sizes and temperaments of these dolphins with unabashed and satisfied obsession, it sort of . . . makes us care?

Nobody ever met a passionate kid and didn't instantly fall in brain love with them. It's exciting to be around excited people! So whatever you're into? Be into it proudly. Own it.

By nannying three wildly different children, what I saw was that you've gotta define yourself on your own terms. Be true to *you*. To what *you* want.

Enthusiasm is contagious. Being different is fun. I'd get such a kick out of knowing the six-year-old would get off on a particular Little Mix song, or that the nine-year-old would FREAK OUT at the joke I just read on Facebook. Because they were so unabashedly themselves, I got the total joy of discovering new stuff myself.

Theory: being the most authentic version of yourself is the highest definition of success there is.

When we're not honouring our truest selves, we make poor decisions, and those decisions ultimately make us feel even shittier. Cue, then, more lacklustre life choices. We're exhausted from mediocrity, and anaesthetise ourselves with the cold knowledge that everyone else is doing it this way so we must be okay. Mustn't we? Isn't this low-level misery just called being a grown-up? ·

Sad people make shitty decisions, and no, that's not what being a grown-up is. A grown-up is a person who knows what they like, what they don't, and builds their days around more of the former in the best way that they can.

That feels a little revolutionary, doesn't it? 'Yes but Laura,' I hear you say, '*of course* I wanna do more of the stuff I enjoy. THERE JUST ISN'T TIME. There's never enough time!'

I wonder how much more time we'd all have if we could forfeit the stuff we *don't* like.

If the thought of a nine-to-five office-job paralyses you with fear – *don't get a nine-to-five office-job*. Quit the one you've got, or resolve to find the joy in it if you can't. Figure out part-time hours or flexi-time, or if different responsibilities would alter your enjoyment of the role. If you hate SoulCycle, don't bloody SoulCycle. Do pilates or get a personal trainer or download a 10k training app and hit the route around the park instead. Hate brogues? Throw 'em in the trash and bring platform heels back. You don't have to drop forty quid on brunch, get a Master's just in case, or say yes to the proposal because you're the only friend on Instagram without a wedding hashtag.

Forfeit the stuff you don't like.

You can be single or in an open relationship.

Own six homes or just the bag on your back.

Make your money in landscape architecture, or high finance.

You can have a kid if you want. Or not.

You can wake up at 6 a.m. every single day, or sleep till noon.

Take your water half-fizzy, half-flat.

Start your days with a fan dance in a pair of fucking nipple tassels, if you like. I'd love to know the secret to getting them to draw circles in the air that way.

Forfeit the stuff you don't like.

And if you like it – if it feels good, and you're not hurting anybody – get on with the business of liking it. Swim in it. Obsess your tits off, sunshine. The world needs more people willing to go all in on what they're into. The world needs more of that kind of love.

Kids are brave about who they are and what they love. Sebastian knows every Pokémon and its worth, in ascending order. Emma owns every single book in The Babysitter Club series, including the special editions and subsequent TV series on both Blu-ray and DVD. Rasheed collects sea pebbles, and every time he goes to the beach has to spend at least three hours scouring the shoreline for the smoothest, most lovely ones. I remember geeking out on some Greek theatre we'd been to see as a class at school, and how I found a note afterwards between two 'friends' saying how weird it was that I got excited. My mate Dan went through a Chas & Dave phase aged eight, with mail-order albums and everything.

So, yeah, brave is absolutely the right word for this, because in this life it's not easy to be honest. Being honest about who you are – getting to know yourself in the first place, I guess – it takes time and patience and will change, over and over again. The essence, though, of knowing yourself comes down to owning the stuff that you love, and not playing make-believe with the stuff that you don't.

I always use this as an example for myself when I'm nervous about coming across as a bit of a dickhead. Because, that's my worry: that if I shout about what I love 'too' loudly ('too' anything: happily, excitedly, enthusiastically . . .) people will think I'm a nob. That's such a 1980s housewife thing to worry about – 'What will the neighbours say?' – and yet, that is where my brain goes.

Anyway.

I very much enjoy spending swathes of time editing iPhone photos with a series of apps. When I was in India, training to be a yoga teacher, a passing comment about how I could later 'Get a little F2 action on that' to a fellow yogi cemented a friendship that will probably last the rest of my life. 'YOU TALK VSCO?!' she squealed. Nobody else understood that she was talking about a very specific app, and it didn't matter. Your vibe attracts your tribe, so you've got to keep it real about what you love, else it just doesn't work. We're still friends to this day.

Related to that, here's a truth bomb: we need to stop spending time with people who make us feel bad for who we are. What we do. People who make us feel bad for what makes our hearts sing.

When a child says, 'You're not my best friend any more!' what they mean is, 'I don't feel good around you.' Fucking hell – oh to be able to spend less time with the folks who do not make me feel like I could scale the moon if I wanted! All of us have people in our lives who seem to delight, even in only the slightest ways, in our miseries over our happiness. Forgive them their own unhappiness and ditch 'em.

Realising that I do not have to hang out with that one friend who makes me the punchline to most of his jokes was one of the single most freeing realisations of my early adulthood, and only last year I had to cut loose on a 'friendship' where the driving force was jealousy and deliberate misunderstanding.

I'm considered the 'wanky one' among my friendship group: the one talking about star signs and the universe and this really great peach she ate yesterday. Some of the stuff my mates get, a lot of it they don't: but that doesn't matter. The good ones *respect* who I am. *That's* friendship. They encourage me to be *more* wanky, if that's what makes me happy. (It does.)

It's just like we do for kids – we buy them the dinosaur books and the ancient Egypt DVDs and take them to the airport to look out over the runway at the planes, because it's lovely to hear them *oooo* and *aaaaaaaa* that way. Lovely to see them so in their element.

We encourage kids to be little weirdos, so let's be little weirdos ourselves. The right ones will love us because of it, not in spite of. And if they don't? Well. At least we're enjoying ourselves.

12

some things I will tell my own children, and hope they tell their children too

I present these in the same stream of consciousness that I give them to my mates at the pub, three pinot noirs in:

We don't get to live the same year twenty times in a row and call it a life. We call that waiting to die.

The pain of discipline is far less than the pain of regret. Get your ass on the chair and go do the thing you said you were gonna do. Be incredible.

We are worthy of every want and need and hope and desire we have. It's our secrets that define us, so own every last part of yourself, warts-and-all, because every part of you is a masterpiece. Even the part of you that forgets to call Mum, and spends most of the working day on Facebook, and sometimes doesn't shower the whole weekend.

To enjoy the harvest, you've got to plant some seeds. Your life is in direct correlation to the effort you put into it.

Screwing up isn't failure. Not trying is.

There are two choices in life: make a living, or design a life. There are 87,987,079 paths to the divine. Drink. Dance Meditation. Sex. Religion. Yoga. Bungee jumping. We're all trying to sample something bigger than ourselves; we just have different ways of getting there.

The difference between what we want and what we're afraid of is about the width of our smallest fingernail. That's part of the fun.

When you allow yourself the luxury of not having to be perfect, you free yourself up to be good.

You are the total sum of your thoughts. Select them like you select your clothes every morning and the beer you'll drink at the bar: carefully, deliberately and with purpose.

We are the story we tell ourselves. Mostly, we believe nobody hurts like we do. Newsflash: we've all been hurt before. That's humanness.

It's okay to live a life others don't understand. Celebrate that. Stop asking for permission to live your own dream. Permit yourself your glory.

If you're not full of yourself, you'll go hungry. You've gotta be your own biggest cheerleader, baby.

Life wants you to be happy. Really! That life is supposed to be difficult is the biggest myth we allow ourselves to perpetuate.

You don't have to fake if you learn how to ask nicely.

It's better to fail in your own destiny than to succeed in somebody else's.

We are wired for love. So let's stop this casual-dating-I'm-just-not-that-into-you bollocks. Let's live from love. From hope. Let's own the fact that every part of us aches to be seen by somebody special.

What makes sense and what your soul needs will often be two separate things. Go with the soul.

Being surrounded by the wrong people is lonelier than being alone.

Nobody really wants to keep secrets. If you become a good listener, people will tell you everything you want to know.

Your subconscious mind will accept any suggestion, no matter how false. Keep checking in with yourself, and monitor the lies you're feeding yourself.

Sometimes everything has to break in the present before we've got the pieces we'll need to build our future. We think stumbling makes us a failure, but oftentimes it's not a breakdown, it's a breakthrough.

Chase feelings, not facts. Your gut knows what to do.

Inspiration is perishable. Do what you say you want to do *now*.

Little by little, one travels far. Tolkien said that.

You do not need to be broken to be interesting.

Do one thing, and do it well. You've either got to be first, best or different to stand out from the crowd. Choose.

Confidence is self-perpetuating. Create some and you'll generate even more.

In the short run few people will notice. In the long run, everybody will.

Never complain, never explain. Just do you.

We're motivated, as humans, by three basic things: reason, love and approval. Identify the emotion you're attaching to any given thing, and it becomes ten times easier to manage your expectation of it.

The more we practise, the luckier we get. Funny that.

LIFE IS A BITCH –
THERE'S NO DOUBT
ABOUT THAT.
SHE'S A CURIOUS,
CONNIVING,
BACKSTABBING
ASSHOLE WHO
RAISES YOU UP TO
SHOOT YOU DOWN
AND THAT'S JUST
HOW IT IS. UPS, AND
DOWNS, AND THE
RAIN ALWAYS COMES
– BUT THEN SO, TOO,
DOES THE RAINBOW

13

improvising

Kids fucking love it when stuff goes wrong – when adults suddenly have to improvise, or go off-script. When the bus changes route and you give them your phone to figure out how *they* are gonna get you all home. When you decide today's the day they can skip swimming practice and go get milkshakes instead. When it suddenly becomes 'Pyjama Saturday' and you don't leave the house all morning, because, fuck it: it's nice to stay cosy and do nothing once in a while. Little people love having a routine, and it's brilliant to them when that routine gets interrupted, because they know *anything could happen*. That's why they ask so many questions. 'Why did the bus stop? What other bus will we get? Will that bus break down too? What if the other bus doesn't come? What if we get on the other bus and that one breaks down too?' Once they know the world isn't going to end (because we are always adamant with them that the world isn't going to end, aren't we? In a way we never are with ourselves . . .), they say: 'Okay, cool. Let's get on that other bus.' Then the excitement can begin.

What if we found the same joy in chaos, in things not working out? What if we laughed about it too? Found pleasure in figuring it out as we go along? In the unknown?

What if we fucking *trusted* that it'll all be okay?

When we forget the key and have to go and wait in the nearby café until the neighbour who keeps the spare is home, we end up figuring out that this new place actually has better espresso than our usual spot.

When the deadline for the big project gets moved up a week, suddenly we have seven free days after it's been submitted, and that's how we end up trying the new yoga studio in the middle of the day and realising that, yeah, actually, Ashtanga is *much* superior to Vinyasa flow.

When the store runs out of the cartons of coconut milk, it's only then that we buy the canned stuff and realise it makes Thai green curry way creamier.

When our trousers split as we bend over to zip up an ankle boot, we're forced to throw on that skirt we thought didn't fit any more but today, for some reason, fits like a glove. All the best romance stories begin with, 'I wasn't even supposed to be there that day . . .' Or, 'It's so weird, because I was an hour late . . .' Love always happens when we least expect it, as does adventure.

I studied improv as a theatre technique for a while, and it's true what all the *Saturday Night Live* actors say: life is infinitely enhanced by applying improv rules to real life – namely, the 'yes, and . . .?' rule.

When you're making shit up on stage, and somebody makes you an offer for the plot, your job, as an improv actor, is to say, 'Yes, and . . .' before adding in your own forward movement to the story. If you're in a scene and a fellow actor suggests that the imaginary thing in their hand is a banana water pistol that shoots out dog poo, you have to say, 'Yes, and . . . it smells like rainbows!' If you were to look at your colleague like he was nuts, shrug and say, 'No. You're not holding anything. What are you talking about?' the scene would be dead. Improv works because everyone is agreed upon the fact that nobody knows what will happen, but everyone will deal with it as the plot unfolds.

If that isn't the perfect extended metaphor for life then I don't know what is.

'*The bus has broken down!*'

'*Yes, and . . . we're going to find another one! Onwards!*'

I love 'Yes, and . . .' so much that I have the word 'yes' tattooed on me, now. After I read Danny Wallace's *Yes Man* I went on a bit of a 'yes' binge myself, and *j'agree*: good things happen when you let them. When you say yes to the opportunities that scare you, but that you deserve, they will take you exactly where you're supposed to go. Faith is so hard because faith seldom has tangible evidence that what you believe in exists. But to have faith is to have trust, and you gotta know by now that the whole point of this book is basically to say, in as many ways as I can, *trust yourself, you marvel. Trust yourself and be kind.*

It's funny how we think we can plan stuff. Like, how little do we think of ourselves that we reckon our imaginations, amazing as they are, even have room to concoct the magic of the universe?

A kid doesn't think they can plan the truly big stuff – a kid knows that opportunity is endless, and that there's no way even to begin writing the details to a story of what could be because that, by definition, is limiting. The six-year-old knows she wants to have a bunny-rabbit farm in the back garden, but fuck if she knows how she's gonna go about it. It's all real in her imagination, though. She knows *exactly* how it looks and feels and sounds, and how marvellous it is. The way to take the blinkers off – the way to let life fly with the whole of her wingspan – is by putting a stop to ourselves when we try to tell our lives what her wingspan is. Let her unfold, and be in awe of how big she is. Control less, and experience more. Say *yes, and* . . . and have faith that, whatever follows, we're gonna be just fine.

(Bloody terrified, but fine.)

(We'll get used to it.)

(Let's just call it an adventure.)

14

the importance of adventure

ADVENTURE: *noun, and adjective*. A foray into the unknown. Making your own path. Normally, a new experience (32 per cent), beyond the comfort zone (12 per cent), that is spontaneous (23 per cent), fear-riddled (18 per cent) but also very exciting (41 per cent). Maths skills needed for adventure (-6 per cent).

Adventure can happen very far away from home, on grand travels in cinematic technicolour.

Or, more probably, adventure will happen in a tiny moment alone, fighting a massive but invisible internal battle.

Both count.

Not every path needs a destination. We don't always need to know where we're going: physically, or in life. Improvising when things go wrong is one way to explore our lives, but what if we didn't make a plan in the first place? Or, okay, if it makes you more comfortable: what if the plan is to have no plan? What if we call *that* adventure?

We've got to map out certain things, sure. Willing the mental knowledge and correct piece of paper to be allowed to operate on people is *not* the same as going to medical school and becoming a certified surgeon, nor is keeping your fingers crossed to one day have enough for a house deposit going to do the trick if you keep spending all of your pay cheque on shoes and expensive French cheese. But. What happens if you take a left at the end of the road instead of a right? Even though right is the way you normally go? If you always do what you've always done, you'll always get what you've always had.

What if you can have something different?

Eleanor Roosevelt said, 'The purpose of life is to live it, to taste experience to the utmost, to reach out eagerly and without fear for newer and richer experience.' In short: it is yours for the taking. The world belongs to you, kid.

I found myself saying, one day, to the eleven-year-old, 'It's only difficult until it's not.' I think we were talking about her French homework, but we just as well could've been talking about a stag-leg forearm stand on the yoga mat, or setting personal boundaries, or knowing that three glasses of wine is your limit – you don't *really* need the fourth. *Most* things are only difficult until they're not.

Stepping out of our comfort zone is designed to be scary. The first day of school, first time swimming without armbands, first haircut, first overnight stay at a friend's house. First piano exam, first oyster, first kiss. All the firsts. But, when we step out of our comfort zone we make that comfort zone just the tiniest bit bigger. That's what makes adventure less stressful next time. We're comfortable with more, and more, and more, until adventure is second nature.

Humans are wired to default to the familiar, because biologically we like to – you know – stay alive. But, if humans can leave Africa and settle throughout the entire world without shying away from the unknown, finding new food sources and safe places to live and crossing oceans even though they didn't know what they'd find on the other side . . . well, you and I can both resolve to try a new holiday spot.

Remember how we said you'd pledge to be your own best friend no matter what the outcome of any particular action is? No matter how something new turns out, the important thing is that you stepped out of that comfort zone – and whether you 'succeed' when you do that or not, you practised being brave, baby – and that's a fucking WIN.

And, it's all information.

All experience informs you about who you are and how you look at the world and what might be possible.

You *deserve* as much information as possible on these things.

You deserve to be exhilarated and terrified as you keep on keeping on, putting one foot in front of the other as you head towards your own endless becoming.

New positive activity can feel even better when experienced with a friend. So. If the idea of adventuring – to the latest restaurant on the High Street for dinner, or to Sri Lanka to go and ride elephants – intimidates you as much as it intrigues you, do exactly as every child since time began does and hold somebody's hand as you do it, just like the six-year-old did on my first day of work, tugging at me to try out the swings. She needed me to hold her hand, but it was *she* who made *me* braver, in the end.

A mate, a lover, a family member . . . be scared together. It's a bonding experience. *TIME* magazine once ran a report that any new experience is a good experience, because people who experience 'more' are more likely to retain positive feelings in general than those who haven't adventured at all. Even little moments of joy, like laughing spontaneously with a mate, feed prolonged overall wellbeing. Just getting out there and doing cool shit because you're a bit curious is scientifically proven to make you feel more optimistic about yourself and your life, even when you're back in the familiar.

I THINK THAT IS VERY, VERY COOL.

Interrupting the everyday flow of our lives makes us more aware of the passing of time, too. It's so, so easy to sleepwalk through our days as we live out our comfortable routines. I sure do that: go to the same café to write from, use the same treadmill in the gym every single time I go, call my mother at 9 a.m. and my father at 6 p.m., without fail. Routine can be comforting, of course – I don't know where I'd be without daily calls to family, *just because* – but neuroscientist David Eagleman explains how sticking with the familiar affects how we perceive the passage of time: '*The more familiar the world becomes, the less information your brain writes down, and the more quickly time seems to pass.*'

That's why we think time goes by faster when we're older. It's why we remember childhood summers that went on and on and on, whereas old age slips by: because everything was new back then, and nothing is now.

Make like a child, then, and add some unfamiliarity back into your day. A toddler doesn't *know* what's up those stairs, but goddamn it, they're gonna give climbing them a go. And then look! A WHOLE NEW FLOOR OF THE HOUSE TO WORRY MUM AND DAD WITH! Oh! And see there! I think that's an uncovered plug socket!

Keep your senses sharp and alive. Adventure doesn't happen by accident – it's okay to engineer it. Talk to the person serving you your coffee, sit next to somebody new in the staff cafeteria, book tickets for that play you think is a bit too smart for you but floats your mental boat at the same time. You can be a paradox.

Wander into the church or mosque, just to learn a little bit more, or book the flight to the place you've Googled every Monday night since the beginning of the year. Take a friend to a silent speed-dating night. Swim with the sharks. Ask the girl out.

Be terrified.

Take a breath.

Have the adventure.

. . . It will never not be worth it.

Take a moment to reflect on how what you're reading makes you feel. What does your gut say? What are you afraid to admit to wanting to know, yearning to explore, desperate to understand? Write down whatever comes into your head – even if it isn't in full sentences. Get it down. Write. Start finding the courage to use your words.

_____

_____

_____

_____

_____

_____

_____

_____

_____

_____

_____

_____

_____

_____

_____

_____

_____

_____

_____

_____

15

a short motivational essay about how you're not screwing up like you think you are, so chill, baby, chill

We're all doing so much better than we think, and yet there it is, constantly, consistently: *I don't exercise enough – I'm such a fat, lazy cow. Why hasn't she texted me back? I'll bet I upset him. I'm never going to get promoted. Good things like that don't happen to people like me.*

Self-doubt.

Second-guessing.

Worry.

We can try so very, very hard – with life and love and learning – and yet feel like we're not getting anywhere fast. And that? That feels like failure.

Listen. There is no failure. There is only doing. Living. Life. We think we need medals of honour. A grade for our days. We're so used, as children ourselves, to being constantly praised that in adulthood we feel a little lost without it, and that maybe we're doing 'it' 'wrong'. That what we need is a new 'us', a solution, a 'fix'. *Things will be better when* . . . And we don't. We don't need anything. We are already everything we will ever need to be.

I can't begin to tell you the years I have lost to believing my life would be 'better' when I finally found a loving, committed relationship, when my name was on *The Times* Bestseller List, when my weight maintained itself at a personal healthy optimum instead of fluctuating up and down as though a differing jeans size every day is a cool party trick.

That was the thing when I got burnout. When I was diagnosed with anxiety and depression and needed help to see which way was up. There was an overwhelming sensation that now was terrible, and I didn't know how it would ever get better. Because I felt that way, I thought I was a fuck-up. Burnout made me feel like the biggest fuck-up out there.

A thinker sees his own actions as experiments and questions, wrote Nietzsche. *Success and failure are for him answers above all.*

It's important for us to understand that 'fucking up' isn't failure, that not having certain things – relationships, status symbols, peace of mind – doesn't make us 'less than'.

Stuff changes, nothing is final, this is not the end.

Adults don't ever focus on process, do we? Only end result. Adults define success as achieving a measurable finale (the ring on the finger, the published book, the summer home in southern Italy) but shit: *life isn't quantifiable.*

You can't measure happiness and love and contentment and self-assuredness, or anything else that matters.

We tell children it's the taking part that counts. That entering the science fair even though they didn't get a medal counts, or being part of the losing netball team counts, or that their first love is *supposed* to break their heart. We want them to experience those things so they know what it's like to try and to be disappointed. We want them to know that the teamwork is more important than the trophy, and that 'I don't love you back' won't kill them. We want their skin thickened, their resolve strengthened, their ability to hurt and carry on made better.

YOU are taking part in the adventure of your own life, and that fucking counts, just like it counts for them.

Okay? Okay.

Failure isn't the opposite of success

Success isn't the ability to predict the outcome of any endeavour we undertake. That 1+1 = 2, always. How BORING! How boring to plot and plan that doing this internship leads to this entry-level job, to this promotion, to this 'respected' position.

Success isn't money in the bank or the title on a business card.

It's not followers, or hits, or outfits or colour-coordinated throw cushions.

It isn't a perfect test score. OH GOD! It isn't a perfect test score!

'*Baby, you got six out of ten?!*' we applaud Theodore and Raine. '*That's GREAT!*' Theodore and Raine showed up and did their best. They don't stop taking spelling tests because they didn't get 10/10. As long as you're showing up, doing your best, you get applause too.

Your best is good enough.

Let's redefine success as improvisation. Have you been practising your improv? Let's redefine success as seeing what life throws up and saying, 'Great! Okay! And so . . . next . . .!' like Theo and Raine.

Churchill said success is stumbling from failure to failure with no loss of enthusiasm. I'd add to that: there is no 'failure', then, as long as you keep trying. Being out on your ass, sad as sad can be, and mustering up the courage to stand, and then to take a baby step, and then to keep on walking – *that* is a goddamn triumph. My triumph was stepping back from 'writing' and my 'career' long enough to learn how to breathe properly again. I was SO WORRIED what people would think. That I wouldn't get hired to write books or articles any more because I was a nanny now. But hot damn, you'd better believe those editors saw me living my best life and, once I was feeling better, reached out to work with me quicker than you can say, 'When's the deadline?'

People like humans who talk about their humanness. Who *own* their humanness.

Stopping for a minute before carrying on regardless, assault-like, with a determination to rinse the very most you can out of being alive in whatever way feels good to you in that moment – good, bad, damned inconvenient – **THAT IS SUCCESS**.

Everything counts.

Everything counts.

Everything counts.

Success isn't the accumulation of the things we deem 'worthy' of praise. Success is the accumulation of having sought, full stop. It's entering the next science fair, competing in another netball tournament, dating after our heart has been bruised. Jesus, when did the rules change? At eighteen? Twenty-one? Thirty? To be empty, sometimes – well. Empty shows that we have tried for something. When we don't have anything left to give it's because we've spent our resources on the journey.

That makes us superheroes.

Gratitude and kindness. Self-regulation and humour. Zest and appreciation of beauty, wisdom and integrity, citizenship and fairness. Social intelligence. Perseverance and empathy. That's success. That's human-ness. That's how to get through this mind-fuck of existence. Those are the values we want for the babies of the world, aren't they? Let's not forget their importance in us as well. We're grown, but we still need that 'think the best of ourselves' attitude.

You're doing *great*.

You are enough. You don't need to be anything other than what you already are. There's no requirement for you to operate differently to how you already do, to perform a different role in a different way in order to be received as something else. Everything about you is just right. The bend of your calf and the lick in your hair. The sound of your laugh and the smudge in your handwriting. Your pain. Your needs. What and who you love. Already, you're **the perfect package**.

. . . And so, deep breath: Stop making excuses for yourself.

Put a pin in the story you tell yourself, and others, about the person you'll be *one day*.

One day isn't coming. All you've got is now, and so please, for love of all that is true, go stand in front of the mirror and look yourself in the eye and say, out loud, *I am loved*.

Loved for who you are, by you, delicious imperfections and all.

At the risk of repeating myself: every single action we make, every decision we take, every action we execute, we judge ourselves on. Automatically. The brain is an organised, well-oiled machine, and files everything we do. And to be happy – really, truly operate from a place of love and self-acceptance – we have to tell our brain, consciously, where to file what just happened. Every time. So tell your brain to file everything under *I did that, and I still like myself*.

I said the wrong thing, and I still like myself.

I forgot to take a gift to the dinner party, and I still like myself.

He didn't see a future in our relationship, and I still like myself.

When you know you are loved, that you love yourself, you are brave. When you are brave, you are prouder of who you are. When you are proud of who you are, nobody can stop you fulfilling every dream you've ever had because: GO TEAM. Being your own champion is the most liberating, empowering choice you can make.

Dreams become goals, that way.

One day becomes now.

You start to focus.

You begin to, as my dad says, 'boil the piss off to see what's left'.

Success is knowing how to apologise. Remembering birthdays. Saying thank you. The skill that persuades your line manager to stay late and help you on a project you can't master. Asking for help at all (and we'll get to that, because I know: asking for help is *rough*). If you go off-course, it's about how you bounce back from that.

We don't fuck up by having sex with the wrong person. Losing the promotion. Getting the bad grade. Moving halfway around the world and realising that we preferred home after all. It feels that way. Of course it does. But that feeling isn't fact. What strength of character have you built to deal with those things?

People treat us how we ask to be treated. If we are already apologising for who we are, making ourselves small so that we don't risk being truly seen, the world will respond in kind. We'll be told we're not enough because we already said that first, and the good things will happen to the person who said out loud they deserve them.

Kids ask for what they want, don't apologise for what they want, and if they don't get it they move on to wanting something else. 'Failure' doesn't come into it.

'Failure' is often about blame. 'I didn't get what I wanted because of x and y and z.' Life just is. 'Failure' just is. Carry on regardless. Carry on, carry on, carry on. Everything counts, everything counts, everything counts.

16

asking for help

Right then. Help.

Complex algebra. Drawing in perspective. Getting onto a breakfast stool without sliding directly off the other side. Ponytails, understanding what Grandpa just slurred, reaching stuff. When a kid is unable do something, they do not soldier on in silence, concerned that to ask for a hand might diminish their reputation as self-sufficient and initiative-driven. Kids don't panic about appearing needy, because to be in need isn't yet a bad thing to them. (It shouldn't be a bad thing to us. Needs are okay! As we're discovering!) For as much as Little Mo delights in figuring out how the stapler works for himself, he's also not afraid to recognise when the result is more important than the process, and insist you share your knowledge.

Or, you know, Mo will outsource, and have you do it for him. Sometimes, Mo just needs those bastard papers stapling.

The first thing to remember about help is that nobody ever thinks less of you when you ask for it. That's the fear, isn't it? That admitting we don't know how to do something will make us 'less than' in the eyes of another.

But the thing is, it makes people feel nice to give help. Especially the British – we reckon we're an inconvenience if we accept a hand, but actually, it's quite nice to feel that you've done a good thing for somebody you quite like.

Some things to bear in mind when it comes to help:

- choose the people you ask carefully, and be honest. If they are the people you think they are, they'll have your back
- practise by asking for help from those you trust most, and work your way up to the 'Experts'
- by treating everything like an experiment it helps to make the asking less scary
- nobody goes it alone
- seeking help doesn't make you weak; it can, in fact, make you stronger
- know that giving somebody the opportunity to help or support you is a gift. People like to feel impactful. Think about how you'd react if that person asked you for help. Chances are they'd want to help you, too
- treat yourself how you'd treat a friend coming to you for help. Allow yourself what you allow others
- you can't pour from an empty cup: if you would ever like to be able to help others, first you'll need to look after yourself by knowing when *you* need help

So. Let's start the helpfulness revolution, from both sides. Like oral sex and Christmas gifts, we need both giving and receiving.

First off: start offering to help people. See how it feels. Mean it when you offer. The British, especially, are masters of the empty gesture. Don't be a fuckhead. The best way to offer help is to frame it as 'what would be needed for that to be achieved?' rather than 'what can I do for you?' Make it less 'person-specific' so that the one doing the asking feels less personally needy and more situationally needy. That can make all the difference. Describing practicalities over emotions can be a very useful tool for establishing a more thought-based reflection further down the line. By offering other people help before you try asking others for help, you'll get more familiar with the feelings that can surround needing a hand – even if in this instance it isn't you that needs it.

When people do offer us help, know that for them to offer once is enough. It is not their job to follow up on it if you need that help – it is yours. So, if you decide that, actually, you really could do with an extra set of hands in taking your car to the garage on Monday morning, it's up to you to drop Jill a text to say yeah, you'll meet her there at 7.30, thanks. It is *not* Jill's job to keep asking if you're sure she can't help until one of you accepts or one of you passes through this mortal coil. Whichever comes first. Got it?

Now, the best way to take somebody up on the offer of help is to give them a specific task to do. When a pre-teen is making eleventy hundred paper snowflakes for no discernible reason, they will never vaguely gesticulate to a pair of scissors when you say, 'Babe, can I do something to assist?' They'll set down what they are doing, and tell you how your specific job – yours, and yours alone – is to be the one who puts a small snip in the bottom corner, and then a shorter one above it. They will show you how to do it, and then say thank you once it's done. You feel great, because you know you did exactly what was asked of you. You were the 'two small incisions' person, and you did it *brilliantly*.

Sometimes we've done such a sterling job in demonstrating to the world at large just how capable we are that folks have long since stopped offering help to us in the first place – we've always turned it down. *Proudly* turned it down. That's when asking for help is most humbling (see: when I first had to call my mother and say: Jane, I'm fucked. Totally and utterly fucked and I am scared, and I need help). We forget how to form the words in our own heads, let alone out loud.

Help? we marvel, as if the very concept of it is one we must be imagining. Hallucinating about, under the great weight of the world we're holding. Don't forget that help exists.

Let this be your reminder – you're allowed to need support.

You're allowed to outsource.

You're allowed to say, 'You know what, I simply cannot be arsed,' or, 'I cannot do this yet,' and even, 'I cannot do this at all.'

All of those are okay.

Help is not a dirty word.

Write down what you need help with, and who might be able to provide it.

THINGS I NEED HELP WITH	WHO I CAN ASK TO HELP ME

17

believing in yourself

Kids haven't learned limits yet, and so for them opportunity is limit*less*. They haven't tasted the bitter regret of saying 'I want you,' and hearing awkward silence. A toddler hasn't been told they haven't got a natural head for numbers, or that only 0.01 per cent of gymnasts make it to the Olympics. A teenager doesn't know what it is to default on a credit card bill, nor a tween the agony of forgetting to plan for a period. The ways in which we tell our adult selves that something isn't possible comes from negative experiences. Learned experience. But what if we operated from a place where we deliberately forget those negative experiences? If we had a 'clean slate' like a fearless child? A blank page? What else would be possible?

Look. The way I see it is, there are two ways to do this.

Life.

There are two ways to do life.

There's *their* way, and there's *your* way.

Their way has been done before. It is tried and tested. Safe. Has an almost certain outcome. It's easy to do it

Their way, because the road to where *They* are is well worn and visible. We can see it. Understand it. Other people like it when you do things *Their* way, because it validates the decisions they've made. Reassures them they're doing it right. So *They* encourage it. *Hey!* they say. *Come on in! The water's fine!*

Fine isn't good enough for you.

Trust that you know yourself. That you are resourceful and capable and can go beyond the norm. Tell yourself: *I will love myself no matter what I do*. Are you getting the hang of that, yet?

Doing it *Your* Way isn't certain. *Your* Way hasn't been done before. *Your* Way is unfamiliar, and we don't like things that are unfamiliar because **we've been taught that the unfamiliar is too much of a gamble by the people who can't take a gamble themselves**.

And yet, we love it when our kids try something new, experiment, when they fuck up – because we know they learn by doing so. A kid keeps on becoming who they're supposed to be because we hold their hand as they figure stuff out.

Hold your own hand, too.

I guess the thing is, when you do things differently to the crowd, it forces the crowd to ask the questions they'd successfully avoided.

'Is this enough?'

'Am I happy?'

'What would I do if I wasn't so afraid?'

. . . What would you do if YOU weren't so afraid, cutie?

Okay, here's the really serious bit. Stop waiting for the green light. Quit hanging around for the big announcement that YES! YOU ARE HEREBY GRANTED PERMISSION FROM THE WORLD AT LARGE TO DO WHAT YOU WANT TO DO! YOU GO DO IT!

It's not coming, babe. The permission to love your body, to shout about what you're good at, to love who you want (and how). Permission to do more of this and less of that, to make your own schedule, take control of your own plans, to be able to say THANKS, BUT ACTUALLY I THINK I'D PREFER TO DO IT LIKE THIS INSTEAD.

You've got to give *yourself* permission.

Permission to ask why. Permission to wonder. Permission to dream.

Permission to be child-like.

Kids just go for it: go all out on building whatever they can from Lego, refusing to dismantle anything, because it is 'art'. They ask how aeroplanes work and what a disability is and give their pocket money to the homeless man on the corner because that's a nice thing to do and anyway, they've got more money at home.

Let this book be your permission slip, if you need that extra nudge. That's why you picked it up from the shelf, isn't it? Because a little voice in your head read the blurb and thought, 'Yes. I like what she is saying.'

You're as amazing as you let yourself be. And for so many of us, this is terrifying. Debilitating. So we keep ourselves small so as not to risk the inconvenient truth that we could be everyday superstars, if only we were bold enough to surrender to our true power.

Live large, with that child-like enthusiasm and wilful naïveté of: 'I love Mummy, and I love Daddy, and I love myself.'

I'll do it with you.

Some Things You Can Do
To Practise Believing In Yourself

*keep up that fence around your open heart – everything
you create comes from it. Another reason to guard it like
the treasure it is.*

*be careful what you let influence you – we stop children
from watching TV before school, and limit the shows they
can access on YouTube: we screen the books they read and
are mindful about the company they keep. Be as mindful
of yourself. Don't just consume crap, thoughtlessly.
Deliberately seek out content and experiences and people
that will inspire you and lift you up.*

*know what you live for – ask yourself what your purpose
is. How can you contribute?*

*every morning when you wake up, and every evening
before you go to sleep, visualise your most realised, happy,
whole self. Breathe in how it feels, imagine how it looks.
Know that by visualising it so strongly you're putting the
cogs in your brain to work on making it happen, even
when you're not conscious of it.*

*seek out hearing the word 'no', so you know it doesn't ever
kill you. If you always got a 'yes', it wouldn't be worth it.*

THE THING I AM TOO SCARED TO ADMIT I DREAM ABOUT IS:

_____

18

abandoning what isn't working

A child doesn't persevere with what isn't working out of some stubborn sense of pride. If it doesn't work, they quit!

They move on!

THEY DO NOT THINK ABOUT IT AGAIN!

How freeing.

How freeing not to give a shit about what it means to 'give up'.

When they can't do question six on a biology test, they leave it blank and head on over to question seven. When they can't build the Taj Mahal out of their birthday Lego, they mash a bunch of bricks together and call it 'The Princesses Tower of Freedom in Heaven Where Everyone Gets a Puppy'. It's not giving up when a kid swaps Barbie for books, or gets bored by Monopoly and so starts enacting a scene with the dog and top hat. Abandoning what isn't working doesn't make you a 'failure', because there is no 'fail', remember?

You don't have to carry on when the thing you're carrying on with is emphatically just not coming together.

A book you're struggling with, the unsatisfactory relationship you have with your hairdresser, a marriage or friendship or project or shit cup of tea.

Sometimes, abandoning what isn't working is about being brave, and being brave is often about letting people help you so that you don't have to have your shit together this morning. This week. This month, or year. So stop. Quit.

This book (this life) isn't about faking a child-like enthusiasm for your own existence until it becomes truth. Feigning enthusiasm until you really do feel it.

This is a book (life) about owning your truth, and sometimes your truth is bone-goddamn-tired. Remember what else we said? The thing about sleep? Because it's okay to need a break.

When we're so bogged down in the sludge of our lives, sometimes it is best to cease walking.

To stand still.

Progress isn't always a forward force – progress can be taking stock of who we are and what we've got and what brought us this far.

When the thing we most want continues to elude us, perhaps that thing isn't for us. Not ever, or maybe just for now. Sometimes the thing we want is a butterfly: it will come and rest on our shoulder, gently and quietly, but we have to stop chasing it first.

We have to learn to exhale as much as inhale, let go as much as seek.

(I wish I could tattoo that sentence to the inside of my eyelids.)

Sometimes we have to use hurt, or discontent, or unease – listen to it – in order to inform our next decisions. Slowing down the senses by stopping, or quitting for a while, it helps us to identify what feels good. You know – rather than risking doing things because they make us feel at all. Because, we think busy-ness is a virtue. In quitting for a minute, we know what feels good for real, and we can lean, then, into that. We can hear the guiding voices more clearly in the silence.

Noor Shirazie says that if flowers can teach themselves to bloom after winter passes, then so can you. She's right.

Understand that we must wrestle for our happiness but that the best people aren't happy, they're whole.

That means fighting the good fight, knowing what can change and what to surrender into staying the same, and having the grace to know the difference.

Sometimes the biggest win is the thing we walk away from.

We don't have to cry tears over spilt milk, though. We can wipe it up and forget about it. Quitting isn't a character flaw. Quittin' ain't always so terrible, sugartits.

IF NOBODY WOULD JUDGE ME, I WOULD QUIT:

-
-
-
-

When you don't know what to do next – in work, in love, in life – do nothing.

Just for a little bit longer.

Don't know, be unsure, for a little bit more time. The answer will reveal itself. It always does.

19

you can't fast-forward the scary parts

When I took the kids I nannied to see *Ghostbusters*, I told the youngest one who had worried about how scary ghosts could be: '*Yes, bits will be scary. In almost every movie there are scary bits. But. When it gets scary, you can sit in my lap, or close your eyes, or ask me to tell you when it's okay to look again. But one thing we can't do is leave, okay? It won't be scary for long.*'

I did that because you can't fast-forward the scary parts in life. You can only sit in them until they scare you a little less. The thing is, in movies like *Ghostbusters* the funny bits always directly follow the icky bits. If you sit tight long enough, the good, nice bits come.

Just like in life.

When you're scared – when you're in the darkest of dark – acknowledge that you might not have the answers, but goddamn it you're prepared to listen.

You're prepared to listen to the people who love you, the people you respect, your own, slow-beating and true fucking heart.

Know that this won't last forever – but it might last a little longer than you'd like.

Write your fears down. Keep applying the 'so what' rule. *'I'm worried this book will never get published.'* So what? *'If this book never gets published all this work will have been for nothing.'* So what? *'If all this work is for nothing, it means I'm not talented at all and my whole identity relies on me being a talented writer.'* Ah. So that's my problem. I self-identify as 'special' because I write, and if somebody thinks I'm not a good writer, I must therefore not be special.

When I confront that – write it down and see it in black and white that way – I can see: if I attach my self-worth to something external, it won't ever feel like enough. I won't ever feel like enough.

I must get past my idea of myself to get out of my own way: acknowledge that I remember birthdays, and know which Gorgonzola to best pair with the figs, and am able to do a killer Aussie accent. I can remind you you're worthy by reminding myself that I am too; I can shake my booty more dramatically than anyone else you've ever seen. Those are the things that are important. Writing becomes about my pleasure, then – the journey, not the result.

Once again: leaning into what feels good.

Doing more of that, and less of the other stuff.

You have to smash some things up – preconceived conceptions, ideas about yourself, projects, decisions – to let in the light. (Quit, too. Another reason why if it doesn't satiate you, you can pack it in.) And from the ruins, in the discarded shards of what we thought we wanted, there will be the tiniest glimmer that will catch our eye, if we pay close enough attention. And when that thing catches our eye, we must focus.

Focus on the tiny bit of beautiful in among the wreckage and let ourselves believe, *this. This one thing makes it enough.*

Fake the courage to rebuild until you've rebuilt enough to no longer play pretend.

Pick a focal point, a new reason, and know that whatever you build next will be stronger than what you built before. Repeat this once. Twice. Eleventy million fucking times. Your work won't ever be done, I'm afraid. If you feel like it is you're doing it wrong.

By learning to stay when things are uncomfortable, by refusing to fast-forward the scary parts, we get braver. Now I think about it, that was my whole driving force as a nanny: I just wanted the kids to learn from me – like they did from their parents – how to look after themselves, best they could. How to be the centre of their self-sufficient worlds.

My fears, and the 'So what' rule:

I am afraid of _____
because   _____
and that means _____
and also _____.

I am afraid of _____
because   _____
and that means _____
and also _____.

I am afraid of _____
because   _____
and that means _____
and also _____.

I am afraid of _____
because   _____
and that means _____
and also _____.

I am afraid of _____
because   _____
and that means _____
and also _____.

Becoming isn't easy.

It doesn't ever stop.

There's no <u>end</u>.
It all just is.

We all just are.

It's a beautiful, messy struggle, and mastering it – mastering becoming – gets a whole lot smoother when we know the struggle <u>is</u> the destination.

That is our arrival.

The journey is
the point.

20

the point of it all is the doing of it all

Not everything needs a reason.

Not everything needs a purpose.

Louie doesn't ponder the merits of building a sandcastle – he isn't figuring out the return of investment on his time when it comes to how many turrets to add – Louie just builds it. For hours! Just to see! Because it feels nice to make things!

For kids, there's no end point.

The point of it all is the doing of it all.

Aliveness for aliveness' goddamn sake.

Working full-time days over the summer holidays with the kids, occupying them became a new kind of monster. There was suddenly no homework or swimming class schedule – there was only time. Big, long, twelve-hour days. But like every mother and carer and babysitter before me, I saw soon that the best way to occupy tiny minds is simple: MAKE STUFF. Cakes, dance routines, art with leaves from the garden. We'd pass hours even just doing our nails, with the right attitude and funny accents.

If you want to lose yourself, if you want to be truly absorbed by something other than your own existential angst, make something. Create. Exist in something tangible that, without you, wouldn't otherwise have happened.

Play, is what I suppose I'm saying.

The kids had these stencils of bedroom furniture and, honest-to-God, I could whittle away whole afternoons tracing outlines of beds and cupboards, carefully cross-hatching them in different colours and adding in details of my own. I'm not artistically inclined at all, but wow-wee: I loved it. It was almost like a meditation, but, you know: funner.

Anthropologist Matthew Parris tells a beautiful story about once being in the south-eastern Sahara, in Algeria. He was in a range of mountains called Tassili n'Ajjer – a thousand square miles of treeless rock. It wasn't always that way, though. A few millennia ago it was fertile and lush, a place where people lived and hunted. These people, they lived in the caves or nestled under the overhangs of rock. At night, they painted the scenes of their lives onto this rock, so that all these years later people like Matthew Parris would travel to see them, to understand about how people used to live.

When Matthew Parris and his team visited the overhangs – the painted rocks – they saw the artwork: giraffes and gazelles and birdmen painted all around. But they also saw, further up, overhead, circles of red dots.

It took them ages to figure out what these weird sets of five red dotted circles were. But then it clicked: if you jumped up, high as you could, with an arm up-stretched, you could just about touch the 'ceiling', where the dots were. The bush people had, years and years ago, competed with each other to see who could get the paint on their fingers onto the highest point of the rocks. They didn't only make beautiful paintings as records of their lives – they also, to put it bluntly, pissed about.

When interviewed on the BBC, Parris said that's what made him feel close to these bushmen from thousands of years ago. This playfulness. The playfulness was their humanness, he said – and that made his spine tingle.

It makes my spine tingle, too.

Dicking around, dude. There's a lot to be said for it.

> *'We don't stop playing because we grow old; we grow old because we stop playing.'*
>
> ~ *George Bernard Shaw*

I played with dicking around, to see how it felt. I'd set off on a walk to nowhere with just a warm coat and my earphones pumped up loud, jumping up on little walls to balance, or sliding down the handrails of steps by museums and around the bandstand at the park. I realised that at home I'd happily spend hours watering all my different plants and moving them to different parts of the house. I'll tell you: my broadleaf lady palm has lived in more nooks and crannies of number 61 than a few. When you dick around, you unlock the stuff you're normally a bit self-conscious about. When you dick around, you get out of the linear, problem/solution mindset of an adult and find other, better answers in the world of make-believe.

Rearranging the underwear drawer. Taking everything out of the cupboards and putting it back in uniform lines. Staring out the window a lot. Drawing faces in the sand with your finger. Dicking around activates parts of our brain we don't often access over the age of twelve. In playing, we make new connections in our mind, suddenly unleashing creativity and laughter, engaging us with ourselves in a new way. In my burnout, it was playfulness that was the first thing to disappear – not that I noticed. I was far too grumpy to notice. I didn't notice, in fact, until my trial shift with the kids, when I danced around the kitchen with them to a song turned up loud on my iPhone.

'God,' I thought, afterwards, 'I've not done something as fun as that in ages.'

Here are some other ways of playing that I found help me to chill the fuck out:

- Walking aimlessly, knowing I will never stray too far from home.

- Drawing. I'm a *shite* artist. Like, embarrassingly so. But sometimes sketching and shading with an HB pencil is just what the doctor ordered. I don't have to show anybody – it just feels good to try.
- Cooking. I'm not a great cook, either, to be honest, but I *am* a very good host, and my creativity is engaged by setting a table, introducing people to each other, driving conversation. I suppose it's about making life a bit more like art, isn't it? *Everything* can be art, with the right (playful) attitude.
- Animals. I look after my friend Jamie's dog, sometimes, a tiny little Cavalier King Charles with eyes the size of saucers. She only has to be taken to the *entrance* of a park before she goes nuts and starts spinning in circles, knowing that a game of catch with a squeaky toy is mere moments away. It makes me laugh every time. You can't be grumpy, or mad, or angry at the world when a black-and-tan, floppy-eared pup is tripping over herself to catch a tennis ball.

What things do you want to do,
simply for the purpose of doing them?

e.g. I want to lie on a blanket outside, and just look at stuff. I want to play with the neighbour's cat, teasing her with a piece of string. I want to shred the label on this bottle of wine, and make stupid pictures out of it. I want to kiss. Twirl. Stretch.

_____

_____

_____

_____

_____

_____

21

ask questions

'Why does that man only have one leg?' 'Why is it bad the orange man is president?' 'Why is that lady talking to herself?' 'Is that a girl or a boy?'

We're too polite to ask questions, sometimes. To talk about the elephant in the room. We'd rather make such a fuss of how unbothered and cool we are with the wheelchair user that we end up making its occupant feel like a zoo animal instead of simply saying: 'What can I do to help best?' Our refusal to ask questions makes an ass out of everyone.

Kids just say it: ask for a breakdown of what grown-ups won't talk about, for whatever reason. You can't not answer a kid's question, because, shit: what if they get their answer from that girl Debbie at school, the one who taught them the word 'fuck'? Or the dark corner of the web? Crap. By us not answering their questions they might end up as *Daily Mail* readers.

What I found in answering their questions, as a nanny, is that I started to understand the world a bit better, too – even when I wasn't comfortable at first. In fact, especially then. Voltaire said to judge a man by his questions, rather than by his answers. He was on to something.

My friend Dan, Dan of 'loves Chas & Dave' fame, is a maths teacher and philosophy graduate. He once told me that the Japanese used to decorate temples with geometry problems called San Gaku. The blissed-out connectedness of working through a timeless proportional geometry problem is kind of like meditative practice – a sort of non-Western acknowledgement that there's something eternal and discoverable all around us. Dan concluded this little lesson by saying, 'It's fucking beautiful.'

I love that. Endless wondering and working out. That's how good conversations make me feel. Curiouser and curiouser. Connected. Purposeful.

Wrapped up in explaining why sometimes girls can wear 'boy' clothes, and boys can wear 'girl' clothes – and actually, what is girl and boy anyway? – makes me stop checking my phone, and my brain from wandering, and truly roots me to the child with the demands. There's a progression, with good questions, where you go from superficial to intimate, with both the other person, and yourself. In fact, I was forever telling the kids that there were no 'bad questions' – I promised them never to laugh or tell them off if they really wanted to know something. It all gets everyone thinking. That's why dating is so much fun (sometimes!) – the right questions make you turn a corner and even if you don't want to see the person again, you feel like you've learned something.

On one great date, I did the '36 Questions to Fall in Love' thing that went viral a few years ago. You know the one: the questions you ask a potential partner that are supposed to foster intimacy. *Given the choice of anyone in the world, whom would you want as a dinner guest? Would you like to be famous? Before making a telephone call, do you ever rehearse what you're going to say? What would constitute a perfect day for you? When did you last sing to yourself? Do you have a secret hunch about how you will die? For what in your life do you feel most grateful?*

It taught me how to be better at conversations. You get incomplete information when you ask yes or no questions, but open-ended questions get insight. Questions with 'who', 'what', 'where', 'when', 'how' or 'why' lead to people giving thought to their answers, and it's easier to dig deeper with those responses, by asking, 'What makes you say that?' or 'Why do you think that?'

Asking ourselves questions is a revelation, too.

Questions to ourselves, about ourselves, are fucking petrifying.

Am I fulfilled by the man I say I love?

*Do I actually **like** going on that group holiday with my friends every February?*

This work might make me a shit ton of money, but am I really contributing anything?

Does it matter that I don't care if I'm not ~contributing~ anything?

Does this duck-egg blue paint really work in the bathroom, or am I saying I like it because it cost me £200 to get the decorator in and I'm embarrassed to have wasted the money?

Am I over-eating because I feel empty emotionally?

Am I obsessed with work, or using it to focus on because I'm too scared to say I want a baby?

Do I actually like children?

Once you ask them you find out what your values really are – and once you know your values it's really hard not to make decisions.

Decisions about your life.

About the way your mother speaks to you or your boss treats you, or decisions about what you can't stand for another day and what you want *moremoremore* of.

When you know your values it's impossible not to stand up for yourself, not to be proud of yourself, not to forgive yourself for being brilliant and flawed.

The magical answers to life and love and happiness that we all crave – they start by asking. When you ask the questions, you get answers – and answers mean action.

Basically, there's no such thing as a wrong question. It all unlocks something within us.

A FREE-WRITE ABOUT THE THINGS
I'M A BIT AFRAID TO ASK MYSELF

use this page to write, with as little self-consciousness as you can allow yourself, a few notes on the things you're scared to admit to wondering about. just to see what comes up. just to see how it makes you feel.

22

get feedback

Speaking of questions, one that a kid will never shy away from asking outright is, 'Do you like my . . .?' I cried on the day the nine-year-old asked if she could read me her poem about 'Sunday Morning'. I don't know whether it's because it was so good, or because she was so proud of it. She made something, and wanted me to like it too. She bounded up to me as I let myself in the house one morning and said, 'Laura! Laura! Laura! Listen to this!' Urgh. It made my heart sing.

Kids want approval, and for you to give it to them. Just like we all want! And what's more, if they don't like your feedback? Yeah, it smarts, and they take it personally for all of five seconds . . . then they go find somebody whose words they *do* like.

I teach that in my writing classes – that you are not your art. That your art is your art, and so the personal doesn't come into it. That sometimes, you've just gotta let the droplets roll off and know what you've made isn't for the ones who don't like it.

There will always be somebody to like you, what you make, who you are, and always somebody who doesn't. It's why a kid will be drawn to a particular adult at a party, or a specific teacher at school. Babies receive this inexplicable comfort from one adult over another – remember that video that went viral on Facebook of the crying newborn at the presidential rally, and nobody could soothe her, not even Michelle Obama? And then Barack came over and held her and she stopped immediately, and everyone went bonkers for it?

Sometimes we vibe with who we vibe with, and it's as simple and complicated as that.

Feedback is important – from those we get along with, and those we don't. Feedback helps us grow. But what somebody else says about you doesn't automatically constitute a truth – good or bad – and it's up to you whether to accept constructive criticism or praise, or refute it. That's the perk of being both a kid, and an adult. You get to choose what you let in.

Elizabeth Gilbert wrote for *O!* magazine about her four questions to decide who to trust. Some people, she said, want to give us 'feedback' as an excuse to simply be arseholes. We all know the one person who'll preface a rant with, 'To be totally honest with you . . .' or, 'I'm not being mean when I say . . .'

'To be totally honest with you, you've never really suited a fringe, have you? Hey! You want me to tell the truth, right?'

'I don't want to sound mean or anything, but I just

don't think you'll ever make it as an actress. You need a Plan B. I'm only telling you this because I care.'

'Look, it's not easy for me to say this but he's a smidge out of your league. He's so successful, and loaded! You want to be with somebody a bit more . . . homely, you know?'

I've met a few of those in my time. The ones who use 'honesty' as a guise for 'miserable wanker'. Gilbert says that over time she's honed a formula for deciding who gets to comment on her life. She asks herself:

1. Do I trust this person's taste and judgement?
2. Does this person understand what I'm trying to create here?
3. Does this person genuinely want me to succeed?
4. Is this person capable of delivering the truth to me in a sensitive and compassionate manner?

That last question is especially key if you're sensitive, like me, and like the nine-year-old. If I'm not going to like what you have to say to me, I at least need you to know how to be kind about it.

Feedback is vital in learning how to engage well with both the world around us, and ourselves. Feedback is unavoidable. Feedback can, with the right childlike attitude, be incredibly rewarding. But you get to choose how it comes to you.

THE PEOPLE I TRUST MOST
IN THE WORLD ARE:

_____

_____

_____

I'M GOING TO STOP TELLING _____
MY SECRETS

23

comfort over style, or: wear what you damned well please

Sequins might sparkle, but you can't climb the monkey bars in a ball gown.

Kids wear stuff they can move in, have adventures in, and if they happen to be dressed fancy and end up with a few grass stains? It was worth it, every time.

Nobody cares about how you look when you're having more fun than them. Than anybody. Mental comfort starts with physical comfort, and so wear the elasticated waist, babe. Choose the flats. And put a fucking coat on if it's cold out.

Don't get me wrong – I'm not saying how you look isn't important. I wear lipstick almost every day, rain or shine, because it makes me feel nice. I get regular manicures and the odd pedicure and spend a small fortune on skincare. You gotta do what feels good, obvs, and to me it feels good to have nice skin and nails.

But what feels good for me is also being able to actually eat in the trousers I'm wearing, and not constantly have to fiddle with the way my shirt lies in case, with one false move, I might reveal too much side boob. I have a beautiful, floor-length camel coat that both Instagrams well *and* attracts compliments from strangers on the street, but hot damn, it's a bastard to wear on the bus. I'm all self-conscious and move funny because it gets scuffed with weird marks so easily. It makes me boring to be around, when I wear that coat. I'm more interested in how it's rubbing up against the dirty wall than I am in what you're saying. Isn't that dumb?

We've all seen the cute five-year-old at the family wedding who looks adorbs in a mini version of his dad's tux, but gets told off for skidding on his knees on the dancefloor because 'You'll ruin it!' That's just sad. No little girl should be restricted from climbing a tree because of her Sunday best, no wee boy forbidden from every dancefloor rite of passage.

Caitlin Moran wrote in one of her columns that her daughter came downstairs dressed for a party, or some event, and took it absolutely the wrong way when Caitlin said, 'You look so comfortable in yourself, darling.' But I see what she meant: it's attractive, beguiling, enticing, to be around somebody who seems so physically at ease with themselves.

It's hard to laugh hard or listen well or respond wittily

when you're fiddling with your jewellery or neckline or hem.

I dare say it's possible to be both comfortable *and* stylish, but I'm not a fashion blogger so don't look to me for how. All I'm saying is: being comfortable is cool, okay? **You don't have to be fancy when you're** *fun*.

This all said, kids don't save stuff for best, either, do they? They want the tutu on a Tuesday, and the Spiderman suit every day of the week until it doesn't fit any more. I fucking love that. The youngest kid was mad for wearing either the sequinned tutu she had from Monsoon Kids, or a onesie. Both were a+ fashion to her.

I turn up to write at my kitchen table wearing said red lipstick because it makes it feel like an occasion – and we've talked about that, haven't we? About making something out of everything? So, if you have a special skirt that makes you feel like a princess, either invent an occasion or make the occasion simply that today is, you've decided, princess day. Why not?

Wear the fancy heels or the good jacket if you want.

Life's too short not to.

But wear it with attitude.

Wear it; don't let it wear you.

I FEEL MOST LIKE MYSELF WHEN I WEAR:

- MATCHING UNDERWEAR
- RED LIPSTICK
- ANYTHING THAT INVOLVES A TAILORED BLAZER
- BLOCKS OF COLOUR, E.G. THE SAME COLOUR HEAD TO TOE
- A SASSY ATTITUDE

What do you wear to feel most like yourself?

-
-
-
-
-

24

the joy of your body

None of the girls I nannied ever complained about *anything* with regards to their bodies. Not once. Nope.

When I first took the nine-year-old to the park I almost sobbed in awe (I mean, as already illustrated: she was always making me sob in awe). She had such un-self-conscious pride in her body and what it could do. She couldn't wait to show me how good she was on the monkey bars, and how she could do sit-ups from upside down and slide around the pole super-fast and jump from one activity to another. It really struck me. The unadulterated pleasure of it.

(Even the *word* 'unadulterated' implies to be undone of adult restriction, doesn't it?)

I noticed, over time, how she loved practising handstands and trampoline jumps, over and over, delighting in all the things her body could do.

It never came from a place of 'I must master this or else my body is a pile of wank.'

Every cartwheel and balancing trick was a celebration of having two working arms and two working legs.

It was a buzz for her to discover what else she was capable of, and maybe push just beyond that to see if she might be capable of more.

I know almost exactly zero adults who are like that – and certainly no women. I know there's a hundred and one reasons for that (*cough* *all those websites we know we shouldn't be reading* *cough*) *and* that, in a world designed to make us feel bad about how we look so that we might spend money on trying to 'fix' it, it's a revolutionary act to enjoy our tummies and thighs and chins. But, Holy Obama, Adele and Beyoncé – homegirl truly made me want to try. I started to use the hashtag #laurajanenaked on Instagram, photographing my body in good underwear and occasionally in the buff, so that I might learn to love how it looked in the way that she did. At a UK size 16, with generous upper arms and calves and belly, it felt like a mini-revolution to say, 'this is me'. It helped me a lot. Owning my body not as a reflection of my worth, but as a vessel for it. Feeling bold enough to get my kit off online is a direct result of spending time with that kid.

I started to make note of how she ate, too – the nine-year-old. She loved sweets as much as any other, but she never gorged. She craved milk and cheese and protein like sausages and burgers. It seemed really evident that she fed her body what it needed, without having to have read 867,687 different articles online about how to 'control your cravings' or 'eat mindfully'.

She already did it. I always presumed, as a childless adult, that kids guzzled until they were sick and didn't know their limits. That's what watching *Willy Wonka and the Chocolate Factory* told me. But I found the opposite to be true: the girls I looked after knew when they'd satiated themselves. I can eat a whole sleeve of Fox's Chocolate Cookies, even though I get my sugar fix after one or two, because there's more at work than my appetite. I'm eating because I'm worried she took my joke the wrong way, and I feel overwhelmed by my inbox, and I still haven't got my brother a birthday gift. I eat because I am worried, and anxious, and concerned, and overworked. I eat because it's how I reward myself, and, sometimes, how I punish myself too. I eat for one hundred reasons, but what I saw in children is that they eat only for one: hunger. And when they're not hungry? They stop. There's no amount of white chocolate pralines in the world enough to fill a hunger that isn't physical.

I was the heaviest and most unhealthy I'd been in a long time when I worked with the kids, after my depression manifested itself as a sort of squishy blanket of comforting fat, unevenly distributed on my jawline and arms and belly. I didn't mind – I was happy to be keeping my head above water, even if I was only doing it to eat another three cupcakes. But. Once my mental fog cleared sufficiently that it became conceivable for me to exercise again, I thought of the nine-year-old every single time.

I promised myself I'd never think of exercise as punishment for ever gaining weight, or post Instagram quotes about how sweat is simply fat crying. No way. That's not hopeful, joyful celebration. Instead I would force myself to praise what I *could* do.

I could do a few minutes more than I presumed I could when I got on the treadmill.

I could still stretch in the way they'd taught me at yoga teacher training.

I could find it in myself to go to the gym not only once, but twice in a week, and then three times.

Every tiny thing was a victory. Thinking about the nine-year-old helped me to count my blessings, not my blemishes. I felt like I was my body's friend and supporter, not its enemy.

AMAZING THINGS MY BODY CAN DO:

My body can do squats, because my legs are stronger than I think. My body can receive pleasure. My body carries my brain around. My arms can lift children up for hugs. My bottom can keep me comfortable enough to sit down for all the hours it takes to write this book. My fingers can dip into jars of Nutella, to eat with an apple or a clementine. My tummy can digest food, and feels lovely pushed up against somebody else's tummy.

If it seems like I'm reaching for amazing things my body can do, that's because I am.

I have to force myself to appreciate every single tiny last thing about her, in a process I call 'crowding out'.

I first came across 'crowding out' through Sarah Wilson, who says the best way to add more nutrients to your diet is by eating as much of the tasty, leafy, veggie-shaped stuff as possible, so that there's no room left to pour sticky toffee sauce straight onto a tablespoon, or eat slices of butter on fresh bread.

I ascribe this to body confidence, too: I have to think so many great thoughts about my shape and size and capabilities that I have very little room left in my brain for body shaming or negative talk.

And it's weird, but the nicer I am about myself, the more I actively want to celebrate my body.

So.

Make your own list of lovely, amazing, teeny-tiny things your body is great at. Be as specific as you can. You deserve to regard your body as highly as the nine-year-old regards hers.

_____

_____

_____

_____

_____

_____

_____

25

'happiness' as default

The girls were happy as default, because their every need is met: somebody bathes them, feeds them, gets them places, plans nice things. What's not to be happy about?

If we can acknowledge our basic needs and do what it takes to nurture them, quickly our default will become happy, too.

Actually, hold on. Let's talk about what 'happy' means first. Because, I don't think 'happy' exists.

A certain level of contentedness exists, though, and that's what I prefer to call 'wholeness'.

The best people are those who know that happiness is a slippery motherfucker, where gripping too tightly will somehow make it elude your grasp. But quiet contentedness, and an understanding that it's not necessarily about always being *up-up-up* but rather that *everything counts*, well. That sure sounds peaceful to me.

What if we were to take a lead from the contented kids of the world? What if we were to note their deep sighs after a hot bath and a fluffy towel, or their satisfied belches after a particularly good meal? If we could identify – and satiate – our basic needs like their parents identify theirs, what would that look like?

Some of my basic needs include over eight hours of sleep, a daily workout, and a phone call every day to either my mother or my father but preferably both. I also need a scented candle available to me at all times when I write, a totally spotless house at all times, and a holiday booked so that I have something to look forward to that is out of my routine.

Things that might be your basic needs could be:

silence
you time
whatever qualifies as 'enough' money
the promise of a drink at the end of the day
the promise of an empty bed to starfish in at the
    end of the day
green tea in the cupboard always
fresh flowers in the hall
physical contact
something to read
a project to work on
a dinner date with your best friend scheduled
doggy cuddles
clean linen
a hot shower
coffee.

A LIST OF TEN OF THE VERY BASIC NEEDS I HAVE:

1. _____
2. _____
3. _____
4. _____
5. _____
6. _____
7. _____
8. _____
9. _____
10. _____

Do you know about Maslow's Hierarchy of Needs? Google it. The long and short of it is that all humans have a pyramid of needs, and you need to gratify the bottom layer of the pyramid before you can start building your way to 'self-actualisation' (or 'awesomeness', as I like to call it) at the top.

At the base of the pyramid are the most basic needs a human can have: food, water, sleep and warmth.

I know these to be the truest of the true basic needs, because if I am hungry or sleep-deprived the world may as well be ending.

How can you make these most basic needs as satisfied as possible? We've talked about making bed- and night-time an adventure, with soft sheets and an earlier bedtime and something or someone to snuggle up to. What about food? What food fuels you best? What makes you feel good? Are you over-eating to fill a hole something else has left behind? I ask because I am the *mayor* of that particular party.

It's worth noting that Maslow thought sexual reproduction was a basic physiological need, too, so you are absolutely within your right to decree that you need to get laid in order to meet your big deadline next week. You have my full support with that one.

Once these physiological needs are satisfied we can move up the pyramid of needs to stuff that is increasingly more psychological and social.

After the basic stuff there's the issue of 'security' – stuff like steady employment or income, personal safety, staying healthy – that kind of thing. The kid's version of this is their snuggly blanket, or special teddy.

Then there's the social – belonging, love, affection. You know how you're a shit to your husband when you've not eaten properly that day – you won't cuddle him on the sofa because you're in a mood? That's because your basic needs haven't been met, so you can't even think about the social ones. Funny how a cheese sandwich can suddenly put you in the mindset for a cheeky poke, isn't it?

After the three 'base' layers of the pyramid, we get into the good stuff – the esteem needs, and self-actualising needs.

Once we feel fed and watered, and rested and loved, we can think about outside recognition, respect and appreciation. We can start to look at personal growth, and fulfilling our potential.

Basically, you wouldn't send six-year-old Sarah to school on an empty tummy and sleepless night, and expect her to get an A on her times tables test, would you? No. You'd get her rested, and feed her well, and tell her how good she is before she leaves the house. How she's got this, and that you believe in her.

Treat yourself that way, too. Make room for that level of self-kindness. When you do, your default overall feeling might become 'wholeness', too.

26

the importance of textual healing

Every kid has, at some point, a blank-y. A soft, snuzzle-y, comforting piece of cloth that is smooth as silk to the touch, and can be rubbed on noses and mouths and cheeks and arms to soothe and reassure.

Every kid also has a good pair of fluffy socks or slippers, a stuffed toy, and good, fuzzy gloves.

Basically, they always have something to hand that is stroke-able, because to stroke things is to soothe and to soothe is to feel calm – and we all like to feel calm. It's why we're so much drawn to owning a cat, or dog: there's something meditative about texture and stroking and nuzzling. It's just . . . nice.

I don't actually have the most enormous amount to say about this, save for the fact that, working with kids, it was a thing that struck me as immovably important. A safety blanket.

My best friend actually still has her childhood safety blanket, and a bit of research reveals that this is not at all unusual. A lot of adults have this 'transitional' object.

Travelodge surveyed 6,000 adults and found 35 per cent admitted to sleeping with a stuffed animal, which puts a 'stuffed snuggly buddy' way more into the mainstream than we'd first think.

A study in the *Journal of Consulting and Clinical Psychology* said that kids who take a beloved blankie or stuffed toy to the doctor's with them experience less distress, as measured by blood pressure and heart rate, than those who don't. Sometimes, you don't even physically have to have the object – just knowing where it is, even as an adult, can provide reassurance. I know, for example, that 'Nanu', my giant stuffed bear named after the doctor who gave it to me when I was nine and broke both bones in my forearm, is in my parents' house, safe and sound. As long as I know she's still there, I'm good.

Doing a bit more research into this, because it fucking fascinates me how a dodgy, moth-eaten bear or blankie can be so bastard reassuring, I found that, apparently, it's called 'essentialism' – that there's an idea that objects are more than just their physical properties. Objects can be inherently emotional – like a wedding ring. It's not the ring itself we are attached to, but what it signifies. Nanu signifies to me, innocence and reassurance and healing.

We attach meaning to objects from a very early age – as early as three years old. A study of three- to six-year-old kids found that 25 per cent of them refused to swap their toy for an exact copy – they wanted *their* toy. Their specific one. Most of the kids that swapped for a copy wanted their original back right away. In a 2010 study, adults were asked to cut up photographs of a treasured item, and even that led to measurable changes to the sweat production on their skin. It made them agitated. We like stuff – we're just built that way. It's okay.

What we touch can be an extension of us – we feel ownership over it. We can hold on to something that connects us or roots us to who we were, reminding us of the work it took us to be who we've become.

In short: keep refusing to give up that childhood toy. You're better for it. Everyone thinks they're the only nutjob who does it, but we all do.

27

speaking truths

It might sting for a second, but kids don't mince their words when it comes to honesty.

'I don't like my birthday present.'

'Your boobies look weird in that.'

'It smells funny in here.'

Telling the truth is freeing, which is why kids aren't pulled down by the burden of a million tiny lies, wearing away their morale. They don't have to keep track of what excuse they told Gabrielle for skipping drinks this Friday night, or figure out a way to 'lose' the hideous bathing trunks their wife bought them for an upcoming vacation. They're upfront about (almost) everything, and what's the big deal with that?

Everyone knows an arsehole who habitually tells anyone who'll listen, 'Me? Oh, I just say it like it is.' These are the people without many friends, who foster opinions as a guise for asking for attention, because they don't know how to be vulnerable enough to be themselves. That's not what I'm encouraging here. No way.

When we say 'speaking the truth' it's simply an invitation to the other person to trust you.

A kid won't worry that if they say your tits look bonkers in the strappy thing, you'll love them less. You asked, didn't you? If you wanted feedback or reassurance you should've asked the question differently – you should've said, 'Can you tell me I look beautiful so that I might feel it?' If you asked a truthful question, the answer will be truthful. But. You know. That's okay! NONE OF THIS IS PERSONAL!!!! How many times will we come back to that?

Being lied to is personal, though. It is one of the most upsetting feelings in the world.

The most infuriated the nine-year-old made me was on the only occasion when she *did* lie. Bent the truth, because she couldn't be arsed to do what I asked. She told me she'd taken her swimming stuff upstairs to her room, and hung it out to dry. I asked her directly, 'Did you hang it out to dry?' She said yes. Two days later, when she needed it again, I found it still crumpled up and damp in her bag. I guess she thought the swimsuit fairy would do it.

'First thing!' I said to her, voice shaking with anger. 'Now you're going to smell like a wet dog at swimming practice, and everyone will know you as the girl who smells funny because she doesn't let her costume dry. And you're going to have to dry yourself on a damp towel now – that's not going to feel very nice!' I grew into my theme. 'But more than that, babe – I asked you outright if you'd done it, and you lied to me. You looked me in the eye and said you'd done something you hadn't, and now every time I ask you something I'm going to have to check you're telling me the truth. That sucks, man! I thought we respected each other more than that.'

Yeah, I laid it on pretty thick. I'd always had such an honest dynamic with the middle child, you see – she was always the one most likely to be ready on time, with everything she needed and a smile on her face. It genuinely hurt me that she'd fibbed. ANYWAY. I found myself adding, 'Babe, I've never lied to you, not once!' Which, in itself might be a little bit of a lie, but it got me to thinking: okay, what other little lies do I tell?

While we might not be able to control other people fibbing to us, we can control the fibs we dish out. Even just a 'fine, thanks!' to a query into how we are today can be a lie if actually we're dying a little inside.

What's the worst that can happen if you speak your truth?

You are well within your right to give your opinion – heck! To *have* an opinion!

Don't swallow what doesn't feel good (pahahaha) – if you're holding back on saying something, the back of your throat will tell you so.

If you can't speak it, write it, but however you deliver what you have to say, do it with love. Compassion. That won't control how the other person hears it, but when their cloud of anger clears, they'll be able to understand you said the difficult thing as kindly as you could, and that counts for a lot.

Just . . .

Don't lie, man.

It's not worth it.

It's not worth how it makes you feel, and how it makes the other person feel when they inevitably find out.

Wet swimsuits and damp towels will always be discovered, you know?

It is normal to have opinions, and needs, and dreams.
It is normal to have opinions, and needs, and dreams.
It is normal to have opinions, and needs, and dreams.
It is normal to have opinions, and needs, and dreams.
It is normal to have opinions, and needs, and dreams.
It is normal to have opinions, and needs, and dreams.
It is normal to have opinions, and needs, and dreams.
It is normal to have opinions, and needs, and dreams.
It is normal to have opinions, and needs, and dreams.
It is normal to have opinions, and needs, and dreams.
It is normal to have opinions, and needs, and dreams.

28

the only thing that matters is now

If you look after the now, tomorrow will look after itself . . . and right now is all about this game, or great dessert, or hug. Everything else can wait – and it will.

Most distractions can be filed under 'past' or 'future'. For example, replying to texts or emails – something you 'should've done' already – is a 'past' distraction.

Thinking about who you need to talk to, the errands you have to run, the things you need to check off your list, these are 'future' distractions.

What matters right now, is now.

It's magical, really, watching a child colour in their art project, or play 'shopping day' with their American Girl doll. I could lose scores of minutes at a time watching the youngest kid organise the furniture so that we could play 'schools'. We adults can replicate that focus by taking some big old breaths, clearing our minds and applying ourselves to whatever is at hand. One thing at a time. My BFF and I, we call it eating the elephant. The only way to eat an elephant is one bite at a time – so focus on what you're chewing at this exact moment.

When we're present in the moment, what we see becomes clearer, what we feel can be deeper.

All of our creative power happens in the now. The thoughts we have, the beliefs and expectations we cultivate, it's all in the moment.

If you resolve to run a marathon, all you can do towards that is this training run, in this moment, right now.

If you want to write a book, all you can do is type these words, at this moment, right now.

If you want to do anything, all you can deal with on the pursuit is this, here, now.

The Law of Attraction is huge for me, because what you focus on expands.

Focusing on the joy in this moment encourages that joy to grow. If you feel good and have positive expectations in the moment, the moment is a good one. If you don't, it's not. Just like that.

Every moment in our lives is created as it unfolds. We can't go back, we can't jump forward. Kids aren't stressed because this is the law to which they operate – *nowness*.

Worrying is a funny old thing, because all worry does is fuck up the now. Worrying in the present moment makes the present moment shitty; it only serves to create a more negative current experience.

Nothing gets fixed, we're more miserable, and our new miserable reality gets reflected back to us in this misery.

The more we worry about a problem, the worse our worry gets.

You can't un-worry yourself by worrying. You can't use up your worry. Worry breeds more worry! It's one of those things we've gotta try to nip in the bud.

We nip it in the bud *now*.

In the present.

It can be a relief, in the best possible way, to realise that we don't have to fuss over the past, or over the future. We don't have to live three steps ahead of where we are. Our only job has to be feeling good, in ourselves, in this moment, now. What is going to happen will happen whether you worry about it or not. So. Save yourself the bother. Let it go.

What is beautiful, brilliant, absorbing,
about the moment you are in right now?

_____

_____

_____

_____

_____

_____

_____

_____

_____

_____

all we have is now

29

bullshit shame, and how we learned it

Shame fascinates me – it's such a learned state. Kids aren't ashamed by anything until we tell them to be: not of what they want or need or how they want or need it, nor of their bodies, nor of their ideas or their hopes and dreams. I remember teaching at a summer programme in Italy and six-year-old Giorgia losing her leggings at some point in between getting changed for water games, playing water games, and then getting dressed again.

'*Non e importante*,' she decided, taking a seat in class in just her t-shirt and knickers. Show me anybody past the age of six who'd do that.

Shame is painful.

Shame convinces us that we are wrong – really, really wrong – in what we feel or believe or are.

It manifests physically, often, with colour in the cheeks or a hot, sticky feeling under our arms. Shame feels tight, restricting, can make us nauseous and rob us of our ability to speak. It makes us want to hide. It bubbles up, all the way from our stomach.

I was ashamed to be a nanny, you know. I was embarrassed to tell people I was sinking so much that I had to put the thing I loved – writing words – to one side, and work with children. We think of working with children as 'lesser', somehow. Those that can't, teach, and all that. I thought it made me less of a successful writer to need a break from it. Isn't that bonkers?

Most of us are willing and able to see other people's wholeness, but not our own.

We fall for other people's vulnerabilities, quirks, humanity, but struggle to accept that we, ourselves, can be imperfectly perfect. Worthy.

We live, I reckon, in a culture that reinforces shame as a way to stop us from changing the status quo. It makes us feel invisible, doesn't it? Shame. Shame starts as a conversation and ends as a monologue. It's us, on repeat in our imaginations, telling ourselves we are not enough and everybody else is.

Shame is such a learned thing. Toddlers dance to their reflection in the oven door and pre-teens do handstands in public and six-year-old Italian kids walk around without trousers on because it feels too good not to – they laugh when things are funny, and cry when they are in need, and love, love, love. But as we age we get told what is polite, what is acceptable, and it puts us in a self-regulating mindset that means we're forever critical of our actions, labelling them 'good' or 'bad' and judging ourselves accordingly.

Shame is a form of compliance. It enforces conformity. Some of us have been shamed out of our dreams and passions, forced to live as shadows of our true selves.

We know, deep down, that we're faking, but somehow there doesn't seem to be an alternative. We hide our gifts, believing that the world doesn't need what we can offer.

But.

But we *should* sing that song inside of us. We shouldn't be ashamed to be who we are – and we shouldn't feel ashamed that for so long we *have* been ashamed! God – that's a meta-thought, isn't it? That we're embarrassed to be embarrassed? The spiral of it all.

Not to get all woo-woo on your ass (LOL, I'm so woo-woo), but when you start being true to who you are and check your shame at the door, you kinda start owning your power.

And I don't mean that it will then be your job to change the world.

I just mean . . . I just mean that when you're proud of who you are, when you're no longer full of shame for your wants and desires and hopes, you become invincible.

When you're no longer full of shame for your wants and desires and hopes, you can change *your* world.

Losing the shame gains you a whole inner world to explore, boundary-free.

30

dancing in the aisles

Happiest I ever saw a kid was dancing in the aisle of an American pharmacy, and her mama told her to quit it. That was years ago and I have never forgotten it: how the grown-up told her to stop having fun. She wasn't hurting anybody! She was entertaining herself! She was being silly and cute and free! May we all dance in the aisles.

I think it was the mama who was self-conscious – the kid gave no shits. Self-consciousness makes us feel like we're on show; like everyone is watching us. Scrutinising us. We can rationalise it and know that's not true, and yet it still feels like the spotlight is somehow on us.

To be less self-conscious, we have to remind ourselves that folks just aren't thinking of us as much as we worry they are.

Go sit in a bikini around a swimming pool, and you'll soon notice that nobody is looking at your belly or thighs or anything else you'd think to be self-conscious about – everyone is looking at their own belly and thighs and the thing *they're* self-conscious about!

We get self-conscious when we worry others will confirm our negative thoughts. So, when American mama berates her child for 'causing a scene', probably American mama is worried folks are silently accusing her of not paying enough attention to her child, of being a distracted mother. She was most probably worried that somebody would confirm her own negative thoughts about herself. That's self-consciousness.

If somebody called us a blue banana, we'd shrug it off because we know there is no rational or feasible way that we are, in fact, a blue banana. We don't think about it. But if somebody said we'd look better without the double chin – maybe we could stand to lose a stone – we might agree with them, because that *is* feasible, to our mind. We've seen the photos of Kim Kardashian on the scales and know what she weighs, that we weigh much, much more, and so we agree with the negative thought that this person must be right. We need to start giving a mental shrug to both the blue banana accusation and the double chin one, too. We shouldn't give one more weight than the other, because *neither* of them are true, even if one is more feasible than the other.

People with a healthy self-respect don't evaluate who they are on the basis of external appearances or perceptions.

What we're striving for is unconditional self-acceptance in spite of imperfections and faults.

Self-consciousness is stressful, man – who wants that stress when there's so much other stuff that is out of control that will stress us out too?

If somebody does articulate something negative about you, next time try responding by saying: 'Huh, I never thought of it that way . . .' and leave it at that. You don't have to give credence to their accusation by acknowledging they've spoken – if anything, you can make them feel like a grade-A dick for trying to drag you down that way.

Maybe they'll think twice before they do it to the next person.

Here are some ways to find self-acceptance, so that you might find the courage to dance in the aisles if you so desire:

SOME WAYS TO FIND SELF-ACCEPTANCE

1. *Intention*
If you actively decide that a life led with self-acceptance over self-hatred is the kind of life you want to lead, kids' style, you'll shift your mental paradigm from one of hostility and blame, to one of tolerance, acceptance and trust. Understand that self-loathing just does not equate to a satisfying life. By setting an intention of self-acceptance, and telling yourself every morning and every night that you *accept* every part of yourself – the good and the flaws – over time you'll begin a chain reaction that will set in motion a more peaceful life.

2. *Celebrate your strengths*

We collect notes on our shortcomings like we collect pebbles on a rocky beach – it seems harmless, but it weighs us down. We cling to old scripts about ourselves that spell out our lack of worth, and that prevents us from remembering how incredible we are. It's simply a case of clearing the weeds: of telling ourselves what we are good at, why we matter, deliberately and purposefully – in our minds, set down on paper, or maybe even with a professional therapist.

3. *The company you keep*

How we feel about ourselves is directly impacted by the people we surround ourselves with. Who is this asshole in your life who is telling you that you have a double chin, anyway? I think it's time to suggest a 'Free-write'. In your notebook or on a blank Word document, allow yourself to answer honestly:

Who speaks negatively to me? Who reinforces negative self-talk? Why do I allow them to hurt me? Are they just doing my own dirty work for me, because I'm not willing to choose a different reality for myself?

Once you've done a bit of weeding in your personal life, resolving to find a solution to such people's negative talk or give them some distance (which can be as simple as saying, 'I don't feel very good about myself around you . . .'), start focusing on the support system that makes you feel a million bucks. If somebody makes you feel good, you're allowed to want to spend more time with them.

4. *Forgive yourself*
We only ever make the best decisions we can with the information we have at the time. Hindsight is a bitch, because the information will have changed: but remind yourself, you did what you thought was best. Right. That's all you can ever do.

5. *Acceptance is* not *resignation*
Acceptance is simply letting go of the past and the things we cannot control. That way, we can focus our energy on that which we can control – and that is empowering. You know what? Fuck it. Sometimes faking it till you make it is the worst advice, and sometimes it is the very best. What would happen if you faked total self-worth until you wholeheartedly believed it? Sometimes we have to think before we know: and remember – it's constant work. We have to practise self-love, not simply achieve it.

SOME VERY DIFFICULT OBSTACLES
I HAVE OVERCOME IN MY LIFE:

_____

_____

_____

_____

_____

_____

_____

_____

_____

_____

_____

_____

_____

_____

_____

_____

_____

_____

_____

_____

_____

_____

_____

_____

_____

SOME MEANINGFUL CONNECTIONS
I HAVE MADE IN MY LIFE:

_____

_____

_____

_____

_____

_____

_____

_____

_____

_____

_____

_____

_____

_____

_____

_____

_____

_____

_____

_____

_____

_____

LIVES I HAVE TOUCHED
FOR THE BETTER:

_____

_____

_____

_____

_____

_____

_____

_____

_____

_____

_____

_____

_____

_____

_____

_____

_____

_____

_____

_____

_____

_____

_____

31

dreaming bigger

Dreaming bigger: this comes back to limitations, and not having any. Why can't you be a taxi-driver who ice-skates on the weekends, or own a store but also design dog collars? Steve Jobs' advice was always not to dream big, but to dream *bigger*. No. Even bigger than *that*. Kids know. The middle kid I nannied once gave me an incredibly elaborate business plan for a 'real life books and pets store' where you could read the stories of each dog – detailed stories, in proper books with her name on them – and then go and buy the dog from her special shop. There would be a full accessories line, too. I started to ask about the logistics of that – about how it takes months to write a book, so she'd surely only be able to sell maybe a few dogs a year, if that – and she looked at me like I was crazy. 'I'll have a team of writers,' she said, 'because I'll be at my interior design job all day anyway.' Like, duh.

All you need is passion, and vision. Two people can see the same thing, but perceive it completely differently based on their vision: where one sees problems, the other might see opportunity (. . . remember how we gotta start improvising a little more . . .?).

Bigger dreams are bold. You *could* endeavour to grow your sales team's targets by 15 per cent this next quarter, or you *could* say, 'Let's get our product into the hands of every fifteen- to twenty-one-year-old in the country.' To be bold, you also need to be specific. It's not about, 'I don't think that is possible', but rather, 'Well, if it was possible, what would be the deadline on that?'

Bigger dreams are concise: you need to be able to explain to yourself, and others (when you're ready!), in a sentence. Any more than that, and it's too complicated. Boil the piss off (as my dad would say) and give us what's left . . .

Allow yourself to imagine and fantasise about the kind of life you want to live. It needs to be rooted in your mind before you can make it a reality – it won't simply *happen*. You have to have a dream if you want a dream to come true.

STEAL FIFTEEN MINUTES

Take a second. Imagine you have no limitations on what you can be, have or do.

Suspend all known reality and luxuriate in the fantasy that you have all the time, all the money, all the education, experience, friends, contacts, resources and everything you might ever need to live a life exactly tailored to your desires.

If your potential were completely unlimited, what kind of a life would you create for yourself?

I know we said not to worry about the future, to think only of the now, but for the next fifteen minutes imagine in as much detail as you possibly can what your life looks and feels like five years from now – or even one year from now. The clearer your vision of health, happiness, prosperity, the more clearly you can move towards it, even if you never think about it again. In fact, don't think about it again – don't dwell.

This is for the next fifteen minutes only. Then come back to the now.

When I worked with Italian teenagers in an Italian convent (it's a long story . . .) I had them write letters to their future selves. It was incredible to see their ambition, but also so lovely to see what they wanted to hold on to from their childhood, too. One boy

– who was incredibly poetic – had been struck the night before by a star that appeared as we'd eaten supper. He wrote in his letter that he hoped he'd never forget the awe and wonder of seeing a star appear in the sky – that he wouldn't become an adult so blinkered by the duties of life that he couldn't remember to look up to the sky. Urgh. How's that for a child-like solution to life as we know it? REMEMBER TO LOOK UP!

When you become clear about where you are headed, you can trust yourself more, trust that each step forward is a step in the right direction. Once you've considered your future, you can get back to the practice of *nowness*. It will be easier to be in the present because you'll be more positive, more motivated, more determined to make each moment *count*.

We tend to move in the direction of dominant career and personal goals, dreams, images and visions. The very act of allowing yourself to dream big dreams actually raises your self-esteem.

Make a list of everything you'd attempt if you were absolutely guaranteed success. Don't censor yourself – have at it. Nobody will see this, nobody will judge this – don't judge yourself, even. Don't think about what you're writing: just do it.

Once you've got your list, pick one thing. Decide on a tiny, specific action that you can do today, and do it. That's it. You're dreaming bigger already.

_____

_____

_____

_____

_____

_____

_____

_____

_____

_____

_____

_____

_____

_____

_____

_____

_____

_____

_____

_____

THE ONE THING I AM GOING TO FOCUS ON IS:

_____

32

you're always allowed to blame somebody, you know

There's a brilliant part of Decca Aitkenhead's memoir where she has to explain to her little boy how it is 'nobody's fault' that his father drowned at sea. A psychologist later tells her how difficult that is for a child: to accept that nobody is to blame. So Decca explains, later, that it was the sea's fault. The child understands this. The child has somewhere to put their emotion. It works – he is instantly relieved. He is allowed to blame somebody – something. He can move on, now.

We get bogged down as adults at being bohemian and accepting, all free-love and go-with-the-flow, when sometimes it really is somebody or something's fault. Let's assign blame, so we can move on. That's an okay thing to do (just like it's okay to be angry, or have needs or want affection!!!).

J.K. Rowling said there's an age limit to blaming your parents for who you are. No kid comes into the world as a blank slate, because from the moment we're born we have our parents' past, their loves and lives and losses and baggage. We just *do*. That's not inherently good or bad, it just *is*. Our parents are our spiritual guides for our early lives, and so of course we're informed by them. They're our guiding light, and generally do the very best they can – like we all do. But we are sponges, and we absorb so much of their unconscious baggage without realising it, and it informs our view on the world as we age.

Some things it's okay to blame your parents for include:

> your disillusion concerning marriage
> your overly high ideals of marriage
> your desperate need to get educated within a
>   formal system that gives you a diploma at the
>   end
> biased political views
> distrust in authority
> unquestioning trust in authority
> fear of straying from the norm
> anything to do with religion
> your prejudice
> an aversion to having children, or belief that life
>   will be incomplete without them
> bad eating habits
> lack of independence
> too much independence

inability to make decisions without outside counsel
inability to finance
bad genes.

The thing is, we all get to a point – I reckon at about twenty-eight, all things considered – where we have to both acknowledge who our predilection for fried foods or Thatcherite sympathies or fear of commitment comes from, and decide to forgive them and take responsibility for ourselves. Something can be both somebody else's fault, and our thing to 'fix' or solve.

Forgive them.

Forgive yourself.

Press on.

If you need to blame the bloody sea, blame the bloody sea. But then ask yourself: now you know whose fault it is, what can *you* do about it? (See also: forgiveness.)

33

laugh like you mean it

Kids don't hold back when something is funny: that's a very adult phenomenon. When somebody farts, or talks about farting, they laugh. Knock-knock jokes – they're always funny to kids. 'My' girls loved any joke told with a Texan accent, and the funniest thing in the world to them was mouthing lyrics to songs as dramatically as possible, but while keeping a very serious face. Whoever laughed first lost the game, but everybody always laughed.

Us grown-ups, we like to be 'cool'. Urgh. We say stupid stuff and wear stupid stuff and do stupid stuff, to be 'cool'. We let outside stuff decide what we should do and be and see, and it fucking sucks.

We leave stuff on the table – we leave living experiences on the table – in order to stay *cool*. We play to the wrong audience to be 'cool' – we don't laugh when we want to laugh in case it isn't *cool*.

Cool stifles authenticity.

Cool makes us override our instinct, turning off 'aliveness' and 'genuineness' – and it's aliveness and genuineness that leads to close relationships and bonding times.

Enthusiasm – eagerness – propels you into the new activities your brain neurons demand, infusing you with the positive manner that brings people into your orbit. Holding back enthusiasm is, like, the *worst* side effect of having to be 'cool'.

Hanging out with kids taught me that it's addictive to be around laughter. People who laugh. Who express joy. Everyone wants to be in the company of a giggler. Why do you think Jennifer Lopez has been proposed to so many times? It's because she laughs in that cute Bronx way of hers, and it makes you want to be the one to keep her laughing.

Laughter is heady.

Laughter is what keeps us young.

Laughter truly is the best medicine.

Whenever judgement is in the driving seat, you're not

34

you are special, and so is everybody else

We love kids because they make us feel seen. Those girls noticed things I could never have imagined: they knew that when I wore black, I was going home to write that day, and when I wore lipstick I had a meeting in town. They knew when I wore my 'pointy elf shoes' that I was going on a date once I'd clocked off, and would ask me about it the next morning over breakfast. I once heard the middle child telling her mother about me, about what we'd talked about that afternoon: word-for-word. 'Laura said this, and Laura said that . . .' She adored me, and I hadn't fully understood that. The youngest one: she'd whisper, sometimes, 'Can we do a "fortune favours the bold" day?' It was Our Thing, and she knew it. Even on the days I couldn't see myself, those girls could.

Kids, they make eye contact, climb into our laps, make us feel like – even if just for that second – it's only us and them in the world.

What if we, as grown-ups, made everyone *we* interacted with feel this way?

They say charm is the ability to make both of you feel good. Charm is making people valued, heard, seen, understood. Feeling like somebody 'gets' you is an exquisite feeling; they don't have to agree with you in the absolute for you to feel like there's a respect there, that both of you matter.

Think about the most charming person you know: they smile when you smile, frown when you frown, nod when you nod. They're a mirror to you, in simple, non-verbal ways, and it's not because they're blowing hot air up your ass: it's because they're engaged in what you're saying. That bonds you.

What I love about charming people is that they're not afraid to show you their vulnerability. Nobody wants to be around the asshole who endlessly lists their achievements and accomplishments. That's not fun for anybody but the person doing the showing off. Charming people offer their authenticity and sincerity to a conversation: 'Oh wow? You just got commissioned by the *Guardian*? Wow. I've been wanting to work for them for years. How did you navigate getting a yes with that editor, then? I'm so intrigued!'

Charming people are generally agreeable people – or, if they disagree, they tend to approach it from a 'here's what's the same about us, and now here's what's different about us' point of view. It's so easy to be the contrarian, to point out the flaws in somebody else's theory or suggestion, but to employ an 'improv' technique – 'Yes, and . . .' – can drive conversation in a different direction, with everyone feeling like they've said their piece.

Now, this might be a bit controversial, but charismatic people tend to use the power of non-sexual touch, too.

Reaching out to touch a forearm or shoulder can add a powerful emphasis to what you're saying, and demonstrate a very comfortable sense of self, which is attractive and reassuring.

When you learn something about someone, ask them why they do it, or how, or what they like about it.

Pick up on one small thing they've said and dig.

Most people want to talk about themselves, if only we would give them the chance.

I once read an interview with somebody who declared that the best way to get people talking is to say, 'Oh wow, that's what you do? That sounds so difficult . . .' Everyone thinks their life is a tough one, so by reassuring the other person that their suspicion is confirmed, you're laying the groundwork for them to feel safe opening up.

Charming people already know what they know – charming people want to know about *you*. That makes you feel important. Give that gift to the next person you chat with, just as the little people do when they associate which shoes you're wearing with your plan for the day. Make them know how important they are by listening. Noticing. It's gold. It made me feel like gold, anyway.

This is something I can do in the next five minutes
to make somebody feel special:

_____

This is something I can do today
to make somebody feel understood:

_____

This is something I can do this week
to make somebody feel important:

_____

This is something I can plan at a later date
to make somebody feel loved:

_____

35

being the hero

Every child is the hero in any story they tell us: it was *their* advice that saved the day, *their* idea that won them the competition, *their* suggestion that was picked. Why can't we be the heroes in the stories of our lives, too? In every story the eleven-year-old ever told me, it never would've happened were it not for her. So many of us settle for the role of best supporting actor. Well. No child would do that. No child plays a supporting role. A child is their own superhero.

Heroes take action. We tell ourselves we'll wait until we're ready, until there's a better time, but yup, it's true what they say: the time is now.

Waiting until it feels right more often than not means it will never feel right, because the perfect conditions for *anything* do not exist.

You gotta build your own dreams, or else somebody else will hire you to build theirs (Farrah Gray said that).

And it has to be, well. Now.

Be the person who actually goes to Paris, instead of the one Instagramming photos somebody else has taken under the hashtag #travelspo.

Don't wait to feel brave enough. What even *is* brave enough?

We acquire braveness in the doing, in the pursuit. That feeling of: 'Holy shit! I'm doing it! I'm really doing it!'

When you look a fear dead square in the eye, you show it who the boss is. Standing up to fear makes that fear shrink . . . but we only learn that by practising.

Heroes do the stuff other people can't even conceive of. Heroes run four-minute miles, and build cars. Heroes get out of bed in the midst of mind-altering depression, and manage to make a cup of tea. Heroes put computers into every home in the developed world. Heroes climb the mountain of their own self-doubt, one step at a time. Heroes stand up for themselves.

Deciding to be the hero in your own life gives you a cause. A purpose. We all need something to wake up for in the morning: decide why you're getting up and use it as your mantra. If you have to break some rules to achieve your objective, so much the better. Whoever made great things happen without challenging what we already thought to be true? Nobody I can name.

Heroes aren't always shining sunlight out of their arseholes. Being the hero of your own life doesn't mean you don't get sad, or blue, or disheartened. Being a hero means understanding how to leverage those things for a greater purpose.

Build other people up. Be part of a network. Piss people off though, too! You don't need to be liked by everyone to get where you're going. In fact, if you are, you probably need to work on sharpening up some of your edges. Seek out people also with a different take on the world to you, and use it to understand all the differing points of view out there. Information is power – a kite flies against the wind, not with it, after all.

To be your own hero, you're gonna have to be persistent.

You're gonna have to press on, even when it is tough or inconvenient or tricky or you're tired or hungry or a bit under the weather. Only you know if it is worth it, or if quitting is the better option. But if you want that dog book series and accompanying puppy shop, you're gonna have to listen to much more than just a doubtful nanny. How will you keep your resilience strong? Bold? Heroes hit roadblocks, and figure out a way around them.

Heroes aren't already fully formed – they work at it. Study, learn, practise.

Find the joy in the journey. Talent is worthless without hard work and practice. Learn rules so you know how to break them.

The best news of all is that heroes are better when they're imperfect, so everything I've said about embracing your flaws and imperfections stands tall and true. The best kinds of heroes are relatable and normal and show their processes. That's that authenticity thing again! Thank fuck.

36

scars are a badge of honour

The mark on her arm from practising headstands on the sofa before she toppled over onto a Rubik's cube. The line on his tummy from the emergency operation when he was barely born. The raised tissue on her forehead, *à la* Harry Potter: to a kid, scars aren't anything to be ashamed of. Scars mean something happened – and they wanna tell you all about it.

Beauty isn't in the perfect face. Or the perfect emotional state. Scars can be skin deep, but they can be deeper than that, too. Both matter. Both are beautiful. Beauty is the grace point between what hurts and what heals. Scars show healing – and that's staggering in its strength.

To have lived, and have the marks to prove it – that is beauty.

Scars have stories.

Scars are maps of our past that show a life lived.

Living is an art.

Surviving is an art.

Thriving is an art.

We can be slow to heal. That's okay. We can honour the process of healing, of becoming this new version of ourselves. We can be stronger for having been broken and put back together. We get to rearrange our parts that way; figure out what suits us better. Be mindful about the person we're going to be. The hero we are.

Scars are the map of where you've been.

Collect them where you can, and tell your story.

We might hurt –
but ultimately,
we will heal.

Our scars are
our badges
of honour.

37

make a mess, tidy it up

Rule number one: it isn't bad that you make a mess – it only matters that you fix it when you do.

That's what we tell kids, isn't it? Make a mess, tidy it up. Like when the nine-year-old didn't hang out her swimsuit to dry: she made a mistake. I told her she had. She knew it was okay she'd fibbed – *this time* – and to never, ever, do it again. The same rule went for getting milk on the counter when eating cereal, or spilling glitter: it's no big deal, but that's your shit to deal with. Go get a cloth.

And yet, adults – we're a bit more reluctant to do that. We're kind of . . . addicted to our problems. Addicted to our mess.

Brianna Wiest writes about this well. She says everyone has coping mechanisms. Being anxious or upset can be a defence mechanism – we're the first to crack a joke about how we're fine because we're in a relationship with the guy who delivers the three-cheese pizza every Saturday night, or point out our dreadful haircut as a fight with the lawnmower. We feel like there's a lot to lose in being vulnerable and opening our hearts to what hurts, so we hide it. And that costs us.

Our coping mechanisms help us in the short term, sure – but in the long term they can be incredibly destructive. Wiest says that we have to be more in love with our lives than we are with our problems, and it's true.

Answers appear when we're calm enough to receive them, not when we're off our tits with worry, listening to the battle raging in our minds.

When we feel like our lives are a shit-show, we gotta disconnect and breathe for a second.

Everyone harps on about mindfulness and meditation, and that's mostly because stopping to listen to the sound of your own breath really fucking works. That was the most valuable lesson I ever learned during my yoga teaching training: breathe. If you aren't breathing properly, nothing else can function properly. In a really tough pose, it's your breathing that goes first, and it's the easiest thing to rectify. They also taught me that if I was doing a pose and couldn't breathe properly while holding it, then I wasn't ready for it: it was the ego, not the inner teacher, pushing me beyond what I should be doing.

'Untangling' from a life that feels like an overwhelming mess can be a case of 'where to start'? Start by breathing. With your breath. Stop for a minute. Stop, stop, stop.

My dad taught me my favourite breathing exercise, and when I was training to be a yoga teacher this was the first 'group activity' I led and everyone was proper well impressed. Try it. Record yourself reading the following, and then play it through your phone when you need to take a minute:

> *Stop. Stop where you are and be here. Be here, and be who you are, and stop. Let your eyelids be heavy, really heavy, until they slip shut. Inhale. With your eyes shut, inhale, and exhale. Don't change it. Don't alter it. Breathe like you have always breathed; simply feel it. Observe it, without motion or judgement. Just breathe. Inhale. Exhale. Inhale. Exhale. Feel your chest rise and fall, your shoulders sink. Inhale. Exhale. Inhale. Exhale. Inhale. Exhale. Adjust your focus. Stretch your listening to find the sound furthest away from you. It might be traffic, or a dog barking, or the birds, or a conversation. Inhale. Exhale. Reach for the sound furthest away. Inhale. Exhale. When you've picked out the sound furthest from where you are, come closer. Inhale. Exhale. What is the sound closest to you? The wind, tickling your ears? Your own breath? Can you hear blood thumping in your ears, or the person next to you, or the dripping of a tap, or the sound of the flickering overhead light? Inhale. Exhale. Move between the two sounds. Listen to that*

which is far away. Listen to that which is near. Inhale. Exhale. Inhale. Exhale. And now, as you inhale, imagine you are taking down a bright, white light. Feel the bright, white light snake up through your nostrils and down through your throat, into your lungs, down into your belly. Feel the bright, white light. And as you exhale, release all the darkness inside of you. From your belly to your lungs to your heart to the back of your throat, exhale the dark . . . and breathe in the light. Exhale the dark. Breathe in the light. Breathe out the dark. Breathe in the light.

Consider that your life isn't so much a mess as out of balance. That happens to all of us, periodically, over and over: our lives get out of whack. It is absolutely, categorically impossible to experience total equilibrium at all times. And rest assured: as difficult as it is for you, everyone else is struggling the same. I promise you that much. It's just how much we're willing to talk about it, is the thing.

When I first started to get burnout – which ultimately became anxiety and depression – my attitude was the second thing that 'went' right after my playfulness. I was incredibly negative, which was unusual for me in the extreme because I'm a sunny-side-up person. Always have been. I stopped having the energy to do things, too – another warning sign, since I'm very much an organised 'go-getter' of a woman, who prides herself on initiative and getting the job done.

I wish I had slowed down when I first started to realise these things. But I didn't. I felt like I couldn't. I kept going; I thought it was 'just a phase'. It was only once I was in therapy that I slowly began to unpick my negative thoughts and nurture an element of hopefulness that I wouldn't always feel this way.

It's easier said than done to minimise stress, but it truly does pay to identify the things giving you most of a headache and ask for help with them.

Regularly engaging in decompressing rituals like exercise, meditation and fresh air will help you see the wood for the trees. There's a reason we put kids in a 'time out' for five minutes when they're misbehaving or having a meltdown. It's only once they've been forced to stop and sit in silence, in their own company, on the naughty step, that they can gather themselves together sufficiently to explain why, exactly, they just stabbed their sister in the arm with a blunt pencil, or walloped their brother in the face with an iPad.

It can also help with focus: that's another thing that left me when I was sick. I got distracted easily and punished myself by not taking regular breaks. I was constantly wired, and so sleep eluded me, as well. I wish I'd done more to regain my focus, and earlier. I wish I'd remembered to breathe. That achieving one thing a day was enough. The booking of the dentist appointment, the phone call, the shower or email or trip to the post office. One thing a day was all I had focus for, and that was okay.

I wish I'd forgiven myself for being overwhelmed sooner.

38

you're not qualified

Kids have no barrier to entry. The six-year-old gave zero shits that she'd never ice-skated before: she decided she was going to both love it and be brilliant, and that's all there was to it. If kids wanna do something, they bloody do it. They don't worry that they might fall off the skateboard, or have never written a story before, or that nobody has shown them how to sift flour for a sponge cake. They just . . . do.

Say yes, and figure out the details later.

That's some confidence.

Listen. Life is all about perception. Your outside worth (NOT the way you value yourself, remember! YOU decide that!) can be all about how you present yourself, and that means a little 'fake it till you make it', as we've discussed, on occasion.

Life's a game, but there are a few cheat sheets. There are winners, and losers, and it is possible to figure out how to play the game. It's sad, or it's an opportunity, depending on how you look at it, but there are definitely some tricks you can learn for gaming the 'system'.

Pay attention to the details.

You need something to say at any given moment, so fill your brain with art, politics, languages: by practising your perceptive tendencies you'll always have something to say – something intelligent to say.

Don't tell your boss you loved *To Kill a Mockingbird* if you don't have a couple of actual smart things to say about *To Kill a Mockingbird*. That's just common sense. And if you don't have something smart to say? Shut up! Silence can be very powerful. Oscar Wilde once said that it is better to stay silent and have people think you a fool than to speak and remove all doubt.

If you're not qualified to do something, be quiet long enough to observe what is happening around you and figure out what your next step can be.

Make friends with everyone, so that you've got a network of intelligence around you and people to help you out should you need it. This isn't manipulation, by the way – you must always offer something in return. Always be willing to give as much as you get. Be nice, basically, and accept niceness in return.

There's genuine science behind 'fake it till you make it', you know. If you do something often enough, you actually become it. It's incredibly sincere – that desire to learn and mould yourself accordingly.

Amy Cuddy gave a very popular TED Talk on non-verbal communication – body language, to you and me. Even if you're not feeling your most confident self, slow your breathing (there we are with the breathing again!) and make eye contact. Loosen your jaw and shoulders, don't fidget, smile *and mean it*. Take control over your body and the tiny signals she gives out, until it calms your mind. It will. Actively listen, too. That helps.

Nobody feels competent 100 per cent of the time. Nobody. Well. Maybe Alan Sugar does. But aside from sociopaths, everyone experiences wobbles and uncertainty.

Highlight your competence to feel confident – like kids do, shout about your achievements and accomplishments. Be that hero.

Reviewing a list of successes before approaching a new task can make you feel more confident in general. It anchors your optimism, and when you approach something optimistically you're more likely to do it well.

One last thing about faking it till you make it, or doing something you feel a bit underqualified for? Be polite. Confidence isn't always about drawing attention to yourself; it can be about being secure and rooted enough to draw attention to others.

> **I'm not qualified to do this,**
> **but I want to do it anyway:**
>
> _____
>
> **And what's more? I'm gonna *slay it*.**

39

closing thoughts on embracing your life as the mess it is

As I was writing this book, several friends talked to me about how, when it comes down to it, they feel like they're fucking up as adults because life feels messy. Untidy. Out of control. It's the great lie of our lives, isn't it? That one day we will 'arrive'. Be completed. What came up in these conversations was the conclusion that we'll forever be juggling balls, figuring stuff out, learning and pushing, and never with the laundry totally up to date. Here, then, are some small things we can all add to our day to make us feel like we have our shit together.

- **Write and send one gratitude note**
  *Pick somebody who intimidates you a little –
  someone who you couldn't say it to their face, even
  if you wanted to. Say, 'I read this thing in a really
  useful book about telling people when you're*

thankful for them, and just wanted to say I am grateful for you.' Then explain why. Don't be creepy about it; just tell the truth.

- **Drink enough water**
  No, but really. We need about three litres a day, and coffee doesn't count. Trust me, and every beauty in the land – once you start drinking enough water (and it is almost always more than you think you need) it's like the clouds part and the sun shines down on your life . . . and your skin.

- **Spend one hour planning five outfits to wear next week**
  Being cute and taking pride in your appearance is fun. Planning outfits in advance takes the stress out of getting ready every morning, and playing around with your look is an easy way to start pairing things you've never put together before to really make the most of the clothes you've got. You don't need to go shopping. Again.

- **Decide to make dinner from scratch**
  Keep it simple, invite somebody over to eat with you, enjoy the satisfaction of knowing you made that badass meal with your own two hands.

- **Identify somebody in your field, at work, and ask to pick their brain**
  Tell them you'll take thirty minutes of their time, and you're asking because you have some questions about how they got to do the job they're doing, and need some advice on your next career move. N.B. This shouldn't be the person to whom you wrote a gratitude note . . . that makes it seem like you were just buttering them up.

- **Decide how you want to *feel***
  Not what you want to do, but why you want to do it.

- **Masturbate**
  Like, properly. Think sexy thoughts while you're working at your computer all day, and when you get home look at yourself in the mirror. Take an oil bath, watch some of your favourite porn, and go really, really slowly.

- **Compliment a stranger**
  This terrifies me, so I force myself to do it regularly. 'Hey – nice shoes!' to the girl at the next mirror in the public loo is all it takes. You'll make her day.

- **Go out for coffee with no distractions – no phone, no book, no partner. Strike up conversation with the barista**
  Look up and be present in the world for a hot second, is all I'm trying to say.

- **Sit down for ten minutes on a park bench. See what comes up**
  Ten minutes is a surprisingly long time when you're repressing how you really feel about that thing your friend said.

- **Post a selfie to social media, looking your finest**
  Celebrate the courage it takes to say, 'I feel pretty today, so I am documenting that!' It doesn't make you narcissistic. Promise.

- **Write a budget and figure out a way to set aside £50 per month until Christmas**
  By the time December comes around you'll have your gifts already paid for, and maybe even a little left over to buy your office a round of drinks.

- **Email your boss to ask for an appraisal**
  Does a football manager only give feedback halfway through the season? No! That would make for terrible players! To get better, we need constant assessment, and yet so seldom is it given. Ask for it. Prove you want to be better.

- **Walk for an hour. Anywhere. Through town, through the country, just walk**
  Or, even better: run.

- Ask yourself: what's the one thing you'd do if you weren't afraid?
  Once you've honestly answered this it will be so very hard not to do it.

- Invite somebody out for dinner. Your treat
  It feels good to give somebody a good time, just because.

- Pamper yourself: do the whole shebang. Face mask, pedicure, candles. Shave your legs. Wear something silky to bed
  You deserve it.

- Buy matching pyjamas
  There will never come a morning when you do not wake up feeling 'put together' because of your classy nightwear. Start your days off right.

- Call the person who pushes your buttons the most: the one you walk away from first when you're stressed, the one you forget about because you know you'll be forgiven
  . . . and end the conversation with, 'Hey – you're my hero, you know that?' They'll appreciate that.

NONE OF US IS FUCKING UP LIKE WE THINK WE ARE

40

the takeaway: kindness

Right then. That was *Ice Cream for Breakfast*. I feel a bit funny now that I've written down everything nine months of nannying taught me. Truly, stepping back from my 'career' was one of the bravest things I've ever done. Admitting I needed to take a moment out of my own life to take stock felt like absolute failure at the time, like I was somehow 'less than' or 'unworthy', and yet here we are: I'm 'better'. Wiser. Stronger. Kinder – to myself, and to others. That's what it all comes down to. Self-kindness. I can see straighter, now. See that there is so much good in our lives, but that it is so very easy to get bogged down in shit that really doesn't matter.

I wanted to make a note of the fact that writing is a funny business, and after my first book came out and I stopped writing for a bit, I felt less of an author. Like I couldn't be a 'success' because I was making money from something other than writing, so that somehow removed the capital-W from my profession. How come everyone else was doing just fine? Urgh. My brain played so many tricks on me. I agonised for ages about telling people – my real-life friends and my online community – what I was doing, because I thought they'd think less of me, just as I'd come to think less of myself.

They didn't.

I was wonderfully supported by the people who loved me for prioritising my mental health, and the incredible thing was: I didn't stay away from writing for long. I got to find my joy in it again. It's crazy to me that the thing I was so embarrassed about is the very thing that my publisher suggested I write about – that my editor came to me and said, 'Laura, write us a proposal for a book about what children can teach us, based on what they taught you.' The thing I was mortified by became the next step in my writing. A book! I could never have anticipated that.

I'm telling you this because nobody ever fucking knows what the next six months looks like, or year, or ten years. That's why it was so important to me to write this damned thing: to say, 'Babe. You're fine. You're going to be fine. Breathe. Trust the process.' To say: focus your worry on how to maximise the next five seconds or five minutes. Get more sleep, make your life an occasion, wear your scars with pride. Put one foot in front of the other, as slowly as you need to. Have your "fortune favours the bold" moments, engineered by you and for you. Be the hero of your story. I was in the trenches, too, and no doubt I will be again. That's the nature of our days, the way life goes. Up, and down, and all of it matters. All of it is our story. Improvise when you don't feel in control.

Make the plan be to not have a plan. Go dick around. Be kind, be kind, be kind.

You're remarkable for the way you keep on keeping on, and I hope you know that. I hope you can tell the people around you that they're remarkable, too – remind the people you love how brave they are to be human.

None of us is fucking up like we think we are, is the thing.

When you think you might be: stop. Ask yourself what your inner child needs. Does she need to be told 'good job'? Does he need to hold somebody's hand? Do they need help, or assistance, or a second on the naughty step to think about what they've done? You've already got all the answers you need – they might be buried under all the 'sensible' things adulthood has thrown at you, though. Dig. You're in there. You'll remember.

And if you need a little moment of calm, if you need to look the grown-up rules damned straight in the eye and say, 'fuck you, adulthood', then sod it: eat ice cream for breakfast.

I'll go get the spoons.

acknowledgements

Thank you to many, but first to Briony Gowlett, for gifting me both an idea, and enough faith that I'd know what to do with it. Thanks to Vero and Lizzi for the first-draft encouragements via some very excited Tweets, and Ella for the notes when I was very uncertain as to what we might have here. Liz, nobody at Hodder would know who I was if it wasn't for your first leap of faith with me. Cheers, love. The BECOMING keeps on . . . becoming. What a ride.

When I was the saddest girl in the world, Fern – you came to my house even though I didn't want you to, sat in silence and rubbed my feet. Human touch is vital and needed and says so much more than inadequate words might ever do. It was the greatest demonstration of love I have ever had. Carley – would she have known what to do with me if you hadn't crawled back from the brink yourself? She loved me so well because you let her know the secrets on how. Thank you isn't enough for that.

Megan Gilbride, what you didn't know you asked, what you weren't sure of you gave space, you checked in with me every single morning and almost every single night. Fuck me, I'm lucky to know you.

Meg Fee: always. You're always there, and show up in a way so self-possessed and aware that it makes me better by example. You're a place I've stopped on *my* way home.

Thank you to everyone on Twitter who answered fevered questions about the things they did to relax, or slow down for, or piss about, and anything else I eventually stole to use as perfect examples of humanness for this; and to everyone on Instagram who said, 'Laura! Your adventures while nannying should be your next book!' You knew that before I did.

Thank you to my GP, who took my concerns about mental health so very seriously, and to Arbours Association for dealing with my request for a psychotherapist swiftly and professionally.

Mum, Dad, Jack: of course. You. Thank you for loving me.

index

and being brave enough to
  quit 96
and being a hero 177
and being proud of your
  obsessions 57–8
and facing your fears 102
Fortune Favours the Bold
  Day 13, 172, 198
and loving yourself 82
breakdowns 63
breathing 189–90
  breathing exercises 183–5
budgets 194
burnout 2–3, 77, 110, 185–6
busy-ness 97

C
champion, being your own 82
chaos, finding joy in 66–7
charisma 173–5
charm 173–5
childish behaviour 5, 7–8
childlike behaviour 5, 7–8
chilling out 76–83
choices
  choices in life 62
  making choices 22–9
Christmas 14, 194
Churchill, Winston 79

clothes
  comfort vs style 123–6
  planning outfits 192
  pyjamas 195
comfort
  comfort vs style 123–6
  stepping out of your
    comfort zone 71–2
compassion 121, 143
complaining 64
compliments 193
confidence
  creating confidence to
    generate more 63
  and outside worth 188,
    189–90
  in your body 131
contentedness 78, 133
contrarians 173
control
  and experience 69
  and forgiveness 42–3
conversation 115
cooking 111, 192
coolness 169–70
coping mechanisms 182,
  185
courage 102
creativity 108, 111

experiences 73
extreme reactions 30

gratitude notes 191–2
and success 80
Gray, Farrah 176
grudges, bearing 40–3
gut feelings 63, 75

H
happiness 62
as default 133–7
fighting for happiness 97
measuring happiness 78
healing
honouring healing 179–90
textual healing 138–40
help, asking for 82, 84–8
heroes
and achievements 190
being the hero 176–8, 198
and scars 180
holidays 14
honesty
being honest about what
you want 27
being honest about who you
are 57–8
and children 23–4
speaking truths 23–4,
141–4
and trust 120–1

hostility 154
humanness 80
humour 80
hunger 128–9
hurt, feelings of 32, 62, 97

I
imagination 69, 161, 162
improvisation 66–9, 161
and charming people
173–4
and feeling in control 198
and having adventures 67,
70
redefining as success 79
independence 167
influences 93
inhibition 7
inspiration 63
instincts 169
intentions 51, 154

J
Jobs, Steve 160
*Journal of Consulting and
Clinical Psychology* 139
judgement 171
judging ourselves 81–2

An invitation from the publisher

Join us at www.hodder.co.uk, or follow us
on Twitter @hodderbooks to be a part of
our community of people who love the very
best in books and reading.

Whether you want to discover more about a book
or an author, watch trailers and interviews, have the
chance to win early limited editions, or simply browse
our expert readers' selection of the very best books,
we think you'll find what you're looking for.

And if you don't, that's the place to tell us what's missing.

We love what we do, and we'd love you to be a part of it.

www.hodder.co.uk

@hodderbooks

HodderBooks

HodderBooks